W9-AWR-411

Roger Welsch
is the funniest tractor guy around.

He left a full professorship in English and Anthropology at the University of Nebraska a decade and a half ago to live and write on his small tree farm in central Nebraska. Shortly after that move he was invited to be a part of CBS News' award-winning *Sunday Morning*.

And it was not long after that that he caught the dreaded disease Rustosis, also known as Antique Iron Restoration. Having never so much as changed the oil in a car, he was suddenly and hopelessly attracted to breaking loose bolts, scrubbing filthy engine parts, and nursing self-inflicted wounds. Roger maintains that during the years he has spent in his shop, he has learned two important lessons: 1) he is not an expert, and never will be, and 2) Rustosis is incurable.

Roger is currently a popular columnist with *Successful Farming* magazine, author of twenty-eight books, contributor to Voyageur Press books, including *This Old Tractor*, *This Old Farm*, and *100 Years of Vintage Farm Tractors*. His dogs adore him.

FOR ALL YOU OLD-IRON BANGERS,

BOLT TWISTERS,

RUST BUSTERS,

WRENCH BENDERS,

HAMMER SWINGERS,

LUG SLUGGERS,

PULLER WRESTLERS,

SOLVENT SWIGGERS,

AND TIN TWISTERS, WHEREVER YOU ARE ...

OLD
Tractors
NEVER DIE

Roger's Guide to the Care and Feeding of Ageless Iron

Roger Welsch

Foreword by Dave Mowitz

Voyageur Press

SUCCESSFUL FARMING

AGELESS IRON

Copyright © 2001 by Meredith Corporation

All rights reserved. No part of this work may be reproduced or used in any form by any means—graphic, electronic, or mechanical, including photocopying, recording, taping, or any information storage and retrieval system—without written permission of the publisher.

Edited by Paula Barbour and Michael Dregni
Designed by JoDee Turner
Printed in China

01   02   03   04   05   5   4   3   2   1

Library of Congress Cataloging-in-Publication Data

Welsch, Roger L.
  Old tractors never die : Roger's guide to the care and feeding of ageless iron / Roger Welsch ; foreword by Dave Mowitz.
        p. cm.
   ISBN 0-89658-563-8 (alk. paper)
   1. Antique and classic tractors—Maintenance and repair. I. Title.

TL233.2 . W45 2001
629.28'752—dc21

                                    2001026870

Distributed in Canada by Raincoast Books, 9050 Shaughnessy Street, Vancouver, B.C. V6P 6E5

Published by Voyageur Press, Inc.
123 North Second Street, P.O. Box 338, Stillwater, MN 55082 U.S.A.
651-430-2210, FAX 651-430-2211
books@voyageurpress.com
www.voyageurpress.com

These pieces originally appeared in
Successful Farming magazine.
Successful Farming and Ageless Iron are trademarks of
Meredith Corporation, 1716 Locust Street,
Des Moines, IA 50309-3023.

Educators, fundraisers, premium and gift buyers,
publicists, and marketing managers:
Looking for creative products and new sales ideas?
Voyageur Press books are available at
special discounts when purchased in quantities,
and special editions can be created to your specifications.
For details contact the
marketing department at 800-888-9653.

Historical information in Chapter 18
"The Nebraska Testing Facility:
True Advocates for Tractor Buyers" comes from
C. H. Wendel's *Nebraska Tractor Tests Since* 1920,
published in 1985 by Crestline Publishing.

Photographs in this book are thanks to
George Ceolla, Doug Hetherington,
Chester Peterson Jr., and Antonia Welsch.

Contents

Foreword

By Dave Mowitz

Dave Mowitz is the senior machinery editor of
Successful Farming magazine and Ageless Iron.

Several years ago a reporter from the Chicago *Tribune* called
inquiring whether I could assist her with an article on this
rather "interesting" (her words) hobby of collecting old tractors. "This
seems like such an unusual endeavor," she explained, "that it begs for
an article. I heard you are an expert on this hobby."

"Yeah, expert," I replied, somewhat embarrassed to be described as
such. I passed on the names of several collectors who would make
good interviews in hopes she would go away.

Didn't work. She persisted and I found myself trapped in an inter-
view. Yet it proved to be a delightful conversation, which ended with
the reporter posing the very question I have raised in my Ageless Iron
articles for *Successful Farming* magazine about collecting antique farm
machinery.

"What attracts people to this hobby?" she wondered.

"Well, ah . . . hmmmm," I stammered, searching for an intelligent
answer. Then my brain concocted a simple yet descriptive analogy.
"You know, it's not just the tractors," I replied. "There is something
different . . . deeper . . . going on here."

I went on to explain that antique farm machinery is like fishing
lures. You know, those shiny metal doodads for attracting fish to baited
hooks. "Shiny tractors and whirring implements attract people that

have grown tired of monster truck races, boat shows, or car competitions," I told the reporter. "They come to see the tractors . . . those shiny lures. Then they meet the collectors and *gotcha*—they're hooked."

Strangers to this pastime often wander about tractors and machinery shows like lost souls. Often they come to reconnect with their farm childhoods. Others are interested in seeing history come alive in re-enactments of threshing, rope making, or butter churning. Then maybe it's that "something different" that attracts other people to this hobby. But the heart of the hobby, and the hook that reels in thousands of new enthusiasts to this pastime every year, are the collectors themselves.

Lord help me, I love the people in this hobby. They are the salt of the earth: honest, decent, and hard-working folks as all-American as God, Mother, and apple pie. What newcomers find refreshing and collectors reassuring is that all the people in this hobby are potential friends, eager to share a story and lend a hand.

Antique tractor and machinery people also come from all walks of life—farmers and lawyers, mechanics and doctors, factory workers and airline pilots. Yet you would be hard pressed to determine the profession of an exhibitor at a tractor show or club meeting. The dress code is overalls or jeans, often topped off by a T-shirt proclaiming the love for a particular make of tractor.

And collectors could not care less if you manage a Fortune 500 corporation or collect cans for a living. Yet they're eager to hear how your now beautifully restored tractor was discovered as a rusting hulk of scrap metal buried under the rubble of a caved-in barn.

This pastime is also enriched with a boatload of "characters." You know, folks like the neighbor with two mailboxes, the second of which sits atop a 20-foot pole to receive "air mail." Characters like that fun-loving friend who dresses up like a woman to fool people at Halloween parties. Characters like . . . well, like Roger Welsch.

Roger may have never put on a dress (that I know of). He does, however, wear overalls as his corporate garb, names his wrenches after fashion models, and skinny-dips in the Loup River, which adjoins his farm in Nebraska. This is a character extraordinaire—and also one of this country's finest authors.

I've often described Roger as a modern-day Will Rogers, for he steeps his words in a hearty broth of humor and wit that, when consumed, provides extraordinary insight into experiences of the everyday. Roger revels in the ordinary and finds beauty in the common things like small towns, cottonwood trees, bib overalls, and old tractors.

Nearly a decade ago Roger was fighting high blood pressure and discovered that working on a dilapidated Allis-Chalmers WC brought calm to his body and soul. He grew fascinated with ancient horse-power and began accumulating a fleet of Allises, some working but most in a sad state of repair. Eager to learn more about old tractor mechanics, he attended an Ageless Iron seminar on restoration that I had arranged to be taught by the late Oppie Gravert and his son Jeff.

After the seminar Jeff pointed Roger out in the crowd, proudly announcing we had a celebrity in our midst. "He does those reports for CBS *Sunday Morning*, you know," Jeff exclaimed.

I knew of Welsch's fame, having caught a few of his CBS essays that ran under the moniker "Postcards from Nebraska." Roger was also an authority on rural and Native American folklore and on prairie authors such as Willa Cather as well. Then too, I heard he could be funny.

By this time the audience at the clinic was taking to Roger like flies to wet paint. The ensuing swarm prevented me from getting in a "how-do-ya-do," so I helped the Graverts pack up their restoration classroom-on-wheels in hopes that the crowd would disperse with time. In the meantime Roger had fled the scene, likely in hot pursuit of a tractor that could be had at a price just too good to pass up.

I later discovered that Roger found it hard to turn down a good deal on any Allis WC when, out of the blue, he called me at the office. Those restoration clinics, Roger complimented, were just the ticket for a would-be mechanic like himself.

Did I know he was fond of Allis-Chalmers tractors and must have a half-dozen WCs stored up at home?

Was I the guy who writes those Ageless Iron articles?

Oh, and would I be interested in having him write an editorial on old tractor collecting?

"You bet," I blurted out in unanimous response to his questions.

From that moment on, the hobby would never be the same. For Welsch's wit and wisdom on the trials and tribulations of collecting and restoring old iron quickly earned him recognition as the worldwide spokesperson for the pastime. So much so that I wasn't surprised to receive a request recently from a South African magazine, *Die Veteraan Boer* (The Veteran Farmer), wanting to reprint Roger's original Ageless Iron column and still my favorite piece, "Roger's Rules for Collecting Old Iron and Living With Your Wife." Last summer an Australian collector's journal tendered a similar request. Ol' Rog's humor is truly universal.

By the way, the South African inquiry seemed a match made in heaven—*Die Veteraan Boer* and Roger Welsch. Lovely Linda, Roger's patient and eternally understanding wife, would quickly confirm Roger is indeed an old farmer at heart. Beautiful Brooke, my lovely maiden, lumps me into the same category.

Don't smirk—it's a badge of honor!

Old or young, man or woman, rich or poor, Roger has taught through his wit and wisdom that we are all old farmers at heart. And our emblem is the common tractor, a mechanical beast of burden that may not be as glamorous as a snazzy classic sports car. But through Roger's eyes we have discovered the machine's common beauty.

Beginning with his Ageless Iron editorials, which have appeared on a regular basis in *Successful Farming* since 1993 (and are reprinted in their entirety in this book), and then through a series of best-selling books, Roger has defined the humor and humanity behind restoring old tractors. His raucous celebration of the common tractor as a metaphor for life marks him as the poet laureate of tractor collectors everywhere.

Preface

I can remember as clearly is if it were yesterday the first moment I became aware of *Successful Farming* magazine's Ageless Iron supplements. I drifted up to the town tavern in Dannebrog, Nebraska, late one Friday afternoon, pretty much the way I do every week. We don't have a newspaper in town, so many of the people I encounter at the tavern—most, in fact—don't drink alcohol, but if they're going to catch up with the local news, the tavern is the only place to do it. The usuals at the big table, the social center of town, were huddled over a battered bit of paper, worn to paper-towel softness by repeated and intense handling through dozens of eager hands. I could see it was some kind of magazine, a thin one, and clearly had something to do with tractors. And it was also clear that this tattered tract had captured the eyes and attention, maybe even the soul, of every man (and some women) at that table. Eventually the limp remnant made its way around the table to me, and there it was . . . the very first Ageless Iron I ever saw.

It was of great interest to me because I was just getting started in the wonderful hobby, the wonderful *world* of old iron, but I was also interested as a writer. It was clear that I saw before me at the tavern's big table a reading audience that was underserved. These friends of mine, so avidly devouring the Ageless Iron supplement, are not exactly literary kinds, but here they were, examining those articles about restoration as if they were engraved in stone and had just been brought down the mountain by Charlton Heston himself.

And at that table that Friday night, there was a lot of talk within the circle of readers about a rumor, just a rumor, that this great informational mother lode was not an isolated example of the kind of printed material they absolutely lusted for. No, there seemed to be indications, even reports, that this thin set of eight pages was only a beginning. Ageless Iron was going to be a *series*. There would be more Ageless Iron articles. And they were going to appear in, let's see, it's—yes—it's *Successful Farming*.

It was a bold move but I did it: I asked Mel Halsey, owner of the tattered magazine, if I could take it home with me, look it over, maybe find out who the heck had put this remarkable effort together. There it was, right there in print. It was *Successful Farming*, and the Ageless Iron pages were edited by Dave Mowitz, under the leadership of Loren Kruse.

Crossing Paths

Never heard of them before, but man, they were people I obviously needed to know. (I found out later that Dave and I had crossed paths, although obliquely, in the offices of the *Nebraska Farmer* magazine when Dave was employed there and I was doing research for one of my earliest books. He saw me but made a wise decision about avoiding the wild-eyed hippie sitting on the floor and digging through the past copies of his magazine, and the last thing I needed in my life was some kid who was writing about things like tractors! Heck, I not only didn't own a tractor, I'd never so much as *touched* a tractor in my entire life!)

I can't remember now if Dave Mowitz, machinery editor for *Successful Farming*, initiator of the Ageless Iron series, godfather of antique tractor restoration and collecting, and now one of my best friends, wrote me or I wrote him. Doesn't matter. Thing is, it was a marriage truly made in heaven.

And like most perfect marriages, it had benefits and rewards I could never have suspected when it started. I did write a piece for one of the next Ageless Iron supplements coming down the line, pretty much based on my own experiences in those, my very earliest years in the world of rust and dust. That article stands as the very first one in this book.

Reader response was terrific. I was goofy-proud to be a part of this truly noble contribution to old tractors, history, agriculture, and, for that matter, *Successful Farming*. Letters poured in suggesting that my short history with old tractors resonated with that of a lot of others.

I hoped Dave would ask me for another contribution for the next Ageless Iron supplement. Well, no, that isn't quite accurate, I guess. I suggested another contribution. Hmm, well, maybe that isn't quite the way it went either: I begged to be included in the next issue. Actually, that wasn't quite it either: I told Dave there was no way in billy-hell I was going to let him put out another edition of Ageless Iron without a piece by me in it.

Becoming a Regular

Dave is always one to see the logic and reason when presented in a way he can understand and so he did generously invite me to participate in the series the next time an Ageless Iron supplement was to appear. And the next, and the next, and the next. . . .

Then the real surprises came along: Editor Loren Kruse wrote me that he was impressed by the impact and response that my Ageless Iron articles had had on *Successful Farming* readers. He wondered if I would like to contribute to the general magazine a few times a year, as opposed to just the Ageless Iron series.

That wasn't as easy a decision as you might think. I had a long and warm history with the *Nebraska Farmer* magazine, and a large, faithful readership there. I was concerned about a possible conflict of interest if I were writing humor pieces for two competing agricultural magazines.

I talked the move over with my wife Lovely Linda, always a solid and sensible sounding board for me, and we decided that as much as I enjoyed my years with the *Nebraska Farmer*, the immense new opportunities at *Successful Farming* were simply too enormous for us to pass up. I would have access to a much larger readership—a substantial proportion of them possibly the very people I worried about leaving behind at the *Nebraska Farmer*. More than that, I would be able to work through *Successful Farming* magazine's burgeoning presence on the World Wide Web, another place I was just beginning to explore myself.

Perhaps the real selling point for me was that, at *Successful Farming*, I would be able to go beyond the role of a humor writer; I'd not only be able to write about my new love for old tractors but about agriculture in general, including tall tales, and even serious concerns beyond agriculture. It was the freedom that tilted the scales.

As much as I enjoyed my work with the *Nebraska Farmer*, I have never regretted the move to *Successful Farming*. Along with all the reasons I outline above, the most remarkable factor for my delight with the *Successful Farming* folks in Des Moines has been—the *Successful Farming* folks in Des Moines.

My life has not been like that of most people: I have never really had just one job in my life. Or, as a lot of my pals would surely point out, not a *real* job in my life. There are disadvantages to making a living in ten different ways at the same time: for one thing, as a freelancer (some would say "ne'er-do-well") I wind up working a lot harder for one living wage than most people. And I don't really have any time off—no vacations, no long weekends, no retirement party....

On the other hand, I don't have to put up with much nonsense from any one income source. The moment I get tired of someone's stupidity or arrogance or tight purse strings, I can just move on without inflicting irretrievable damage to our family finances. And my patience with nonsense has grown a lot shorter as I have gotten older. I don't have to tolerate fools, and I don't.

But compensating for that lack of patience on one end of the scale has been an increased appreciation for good people at the other. Even as I become more vocal in my geriatric curmudgeonhood, I find myself feeling all the gooier about those people I love. In fact, I think there is a connection.

I had one long-term business association at the time I came to *Successful Farming* magazine that had been very good for me financially and professionally; but every time I came home from an encounter with this operation, my stomach was twisted in knots. In fact, the two cardiac "events" I've experienced in my life occurred in direct association with these activities. Not a good record. Should making a living really involve dying?!

Feeling at Home

The more time I spent with my new friends and colleagues at *Successful Farming*, however, and for that matter at the parent company, Meredith, the worse things got. The contrast was so dramatic between the "good guys" and the "bad guys," the bad guys just kept looking worse and worse and worse and worse. . . .

I hate to say it (I'll never get a raise talking like this, I know) but the folks at *Successful Farming* have become family: Loren Kruse is the editor who hired me and pretty much runs things. But I have never seen anyone run things in such a way that he seems so totally on *your* side. Dave Mowitz is the sweet guy who is my—*hahahahahahahaha*—boss, insofar as I have ever had a boss, and the one who listens to my suggestions, gives me some of his own, and is generally a dear friend when I need one. Paula Barbour edited most of the work you see on these pages but she is . . . jeez, I don't even know what to say about Paula. She's just a kid compared to most of us, but her sensitivity and concern are so Mother Earth that even this old grizzled dog thinks of her as a spiritual protector. Nancy Nicholas is the magazine's art director and blithe spirit, bringing cheer to the dreariest day and actual, real, genuine art to the most mundane writing. John Walter and Cheryl Rainford run the computer end of things and combine competence with wit and humor; Laurie Potter keeps things humming along at the office and is another important cog in this wonderfully compatible and comforting circle of friends.

Thing is, through their love and respect, I have even more regard for them and their opinions than I might if they were to use muscle. Or tried to use muscle. All too often work relationships come down to "Who's in charge?" That is not only a phony issue, it is a pernicious one. I've seen it, been through it. A good editor (or producer or publisher—or spouse, for that matter) should be a partner in an intended success, not a supervisor or manager. The graceful people at *Successful Farming* magazine seem to understand that better than any other group I have ever worked with. Not worked *for*. Worked *with*.

Past and Future Columns

The chapters of this book are in reality my articles and columns from *Successful Farming* over the past five years. You may notice that they're not precisely as they appeared in *Successful Farming*; we have restored some materials that had to be cut from the magazine for reasons of space. That makes this a kind of bonus issue! Nor are these all of my articles in *Successful Farming*, of course, but only those that deal directly or indirectly with tractors, shops, mechanics, mechanicking, tools.

And there are articles and columns that *will* appear in *Successful Farming* in the next couple years. Thanks to the generosity and foresight of Loren Kruse, Dave Mowitz, and *Successful Farming* magazine, I have been permitted to write ahead of myself, to compose columns well down the line, for the Ageless Iron series or for my column "The Mud Porch," in order to offer you a more complete volume in these pages, a kind of sneak peak at what other readers will be seeing somewhere down the line.

That's a major commitment for *Successful Farming* and yet another example of why I feel such affection for that association. No doubt about it, the *Successful Farming* family is one of those rare corporate entities that you never read about and certainly don't expect to drop into your own life. I never send out my regular prayers of gratitude without a substantial portion devoted to the wonder of these good people in my life.

Readers Are Like Family

But my colleagues and friends at *Successful Farming* magazine are only one leg of a stool with as many as a dozen supports. What about you readers? Hey, you've become like family too! I recognize a lot of names on bits of mail and especially on my agriculture.com Web site (you can reach it by going through http://www.agriculture.com/welsch/index.html and then to the Tall-Tale discussion site) as old friends. Sometimes we get to know each other pretty well—without ever having met.

And there are all my old cronies from here in Dannebrog from whom I've been stealing material, jokes, stories, and mishaps for twenty-five years now—Dan, Dennis, Eric, Melvin, Hoss, Al, Russell, LaVon, Gaylord, Phil, Scott, Dale. . . .

But most of all, there's my family. Son Chris and daughter Joyce are grown, married, and off on their own—Joyce a distinguished attorney—a redemption for that cursed lot! And Chris is one of the best travel writers in the nation—one of the best writers in the nation, as far as I am concerned. I depend on Joyce and Chris not only for stories and laughs but, increasingly, good advice and solid information.

Same with daughter Antonia, at this writing just seventeen years old. She has turned that corner where she is no longer a surly and difficult adolescent who can't be counted on for much more than a good argument now and then and has become a gorgeous, witty, bright, enjoyable friend.

Which is to say, she is quickly becoming a bright wit a whole lot like her mother, my Linda. Long ago I learned not to even try denying the very obvious, unavoidable truth that I steal about 90 percent of my best material from Linda. I envy people like her (my pals Bondo and Eric also come to mind) who have a special knack not only for thinking up great comic lines, but what's more, delivering them with perfect timing and phrased so perfectly they are like poetry. I always struggle to remember *exactly* the way Linda or Eric or Bondo say one of their wonderful gag lines because if just one word is out of place, it isn't funny.

I can't do that. Not even sitting here writing, with plenty of time to consider my diction and phrasing. I just don't have that skill. What I do have are three talents which are darn near as valuable: 1) I have a good ear for what is funny, 2) I have good and witty friends from whom to lift that funny material, and 3) I have no conscience at all about stealing it. And a virtue that hopefully balances that vice is my willingness, even eagerness to express honestly and frequently my profound gratitude to those wits of my life. Thank you, Antonia, Linda, Eric, and Bondo.

Like a Bolt Out of the Blue

I have also confessed shamelessly in my other books and articles to my own utter ignorance about the history and mechanics of old tractors. I did not own a set of socket wrenches ten years ago. Didn't need 'em. I not only didn't work on any machinery, I made a vocal point about the issue. I don't like automobiles, I won't work on automobiles, I pay others to do that, I think automobiles are boring, etc.

Then one day I did some minor bit of repair work on my 1937 Allis-Chalmers WC: a stuck oil pan plug, I think, or maybe a broken brake pad. I have no idea what prompted me to do it. Even though I loved Sweet Allis, as I called that tractor even then, all I knew about mechanicking is that I wanted nothing to do with it. And literally like a bolt out of the blue, as if I had been bitten by some kind of dreadful bug, I was infected with a passion for working on old tractors.

I have given some time and thought to this curious conundrum but haven't come up with much of an answer that satisfies even my own curiosity. What could possibly be the attraction of working in a smelly, smoky, loud, dirty shop on rusted, broken, battered, obsolete machinery? Linda comes in now and then, usually only because she has to, looks around disapprovingly, shakes her head, and says, "So, this is what you do for fun." It's not a question. It's not even a statement. It's an exasperation.

Yeah, it *is* what I do for fun.

At this very moment I am nursing a badly bloodied middle finger on my right hand, directly beside the one with a blackened fingernail. There is a blood blister on my right index finger that screams in pain every time I need a "u," "j," "h," "n," or "m." Thank God I don't need many "7s" or "8s!" There are two abrasions on the back of my left hand, a bad scrape on the back of my left shoulder, and a cut on the inside of my right wrist. At the moment, (knock on wood) no burns.

How can this possibly be anything but an agony?! I don't know how, but I do know this: IT IS. I never end a day as cheered and comforted as I do after a day in my shop banging on old iron. Blood, bruises, burns, cuts, abrasions, and all—it is somehow mysteriously therapeutic.

I have tried to come up with answers. I was an academic after all, a professor of anthropology at the University of Nebraska in Lincoln. It was my profession to investigate why people behave the way they do, so it was only natural that I would wonder about my own peculiar actions. Not a clue. I have no idea why I do this, let alone *love* doing this.

A Complete Departure

I have some guesses, however: for one thing, stuck pistons have nothing to do with dangling participles. That is, my shop and what goes on in it is a complete departure from what I do every day to make a living. Our family physician works on an old tractor, and so does my computer consultant—for pretty much the same reason, I imagine.

What's more, what I do in the shop is of absolutely no importance. Neither is stamp collecting. Or running marathons, or building model airplanes, or bowling. That's why they are so much fun. They don't have anything to do with anything. Oh, don't bother me with the baloney about being in physical condition, learning about history, dabbling in science . . . Those are excuses, not reasons.

Thing is, I can take two years (three, if necessary) to finish up an engine that a real mechanic could rebuild in a day or two. Real mechanics have told me that and laughed at my snail's pace. Thing is, what I do in that shop simply doesn't matter.

The tractor and engine that are waiting right now for my buddies Dan, Bondo, and Melvin to come over and get running has taken almost three years. I finished it last year about this time but every time we started it, it seized up, and so I had to take the whole thing apart and start over. Was I unhappy? No, not particularly. Doesn't matter.

In fact, part of the explanation for all this is hidden in the previous paragraph, in "my buddies." I don't need them, actually, to start that engine and find out what's wrong with it, if anything. I could probably take the tractor out tomorrow and see if it will start, dig back into it if it doesn't. But the point of my shop labors is not, at the bottom, to get it started. The actual goal is *to have a good time* getting it started.

We'll pick a nice day when things are a little slow, start with a cooler of cold beer, sit around and talk a little, look things over, hook up Sweet Allis and her belt pulley to the pulley of this reactivated tractor, see if she starts, work on the timing, adjust the carb, tinker with the mag . . . Before we know it, it'll be time for some burgers on the grill, another couple beers, some storytelling about the last few times we went through this process.

Did the tractor start and run okay? Uh, can't say for sure. That's not what's important.

Still a Tinkerer

The love for old tractors and working on them is in my heart, but the immediacy or expertise of being a real, professional, working mechanic definitely is not. I have learned a lot about tractor mechanicking over the last decade, but I'm still a beginner, still an amateur, still (as Bondo once so contemptuously put it) a *tinkerer*.

So, I owe worlds not only to the mechanics around me who have been so generous with information, parts, and help—Dan Selden, Dennis "Bondo" Adams, Al Schmitt, Kenny Porath, Don Hochstetler, Melvin Nelson, Mel Halsey—but also to the hundreds of mechanics and experts I've never met except on my computer screen.

Especially the good guys at the ATIS (Antique Tractor Internet Services, http://atis.net/) seem to have the answers to just about anything. It has never failed: I can ask the most obscure, goofy, or ridiculous questions and *bang*! These guys come up with answers—sometimes pretty funny, but mostly useful and totally reliable.

I suppose I should also at some point acknowledge my gratitude to my good old tractors too. My Allises get all the credit, and usually my WCs, but there are also a couple Cs, a G, a WD, a CA, which never get the attention nor care they should. The real workhorse here for the past fifteen years has been our International 300. Man, that thing just keeps on going and going and going. I wish I could find a car that reliable. And now there are a couple John Deere Bs, Linda's being the only one that runs (that story appears later), and a cute little International Cub, which I bought because, well, just because it *is* so darn cute.

I am always amused by people who look at one of my books and ask, "My Grandpa has Fords. Would this book be okay for someone who likes Fords and not Allis-Chalmers?" I want to scream, "MY BOOKS AREN'T ABOUT ALLIS-CHALMERSES. THEY'RE ABOUT OLD TRACTORS! IN FACT, THEY'RE NOT EVEN ABOUT OLD TRACTORS ... THEY'RE ABOUT PEOPLE!"

Please, make no mistake. This is *not* a book about Allis-Chalmers tractors. Frankly, I think someone who collects salt and pepper shakers or repairs windmills will find these tales of triumph and woe central to his or her own experience.

To illustrate this point, I once had to take steps to halt the blatant plagiarism of one of the columns in this collection by a *sports car* restoration group! An unprincipled "writer" simply stole one of my articles, changed every reference to a tractor to his own favorite brand of sports car and took credit for it being his own work!

I didn't think this idiot's thievery was very funny, but I was amused how easily it worked: just plug in "Porsche" or "Model T" for "tractor" and there you are. In fact, not long ago, another genius lifted the very same article and substituted "antique organ" (okay, you can cut the smart remarks, wise guy) for "tractor" and it became an article for organ restorers!

Good Clean Fun Packs Appeal

So, the chapters in this book are about tractors, and yet they are *not* about tractors. They are about working with your hands and enjoying a good, decent, clean hobby of putting something right, making something work, showing appreciation for old machinery. I hope the chapters in this book are a tribute to all kinds of tractors, and all kinds of tools, and all kinds of mechanics, and to everyone who's ever had to convince a spouse that investment in a hobby, no matter how goofy or dangerous, is really good for the soul if not for the checkbook.

Would someone who works on Ford tractors or Olivers enjoy this book? Why, I hope someone who restores elevators or hog oilers would enjoy this book!

I wouldn't be in business if it weren't for generous friends like Verne Holoubek (if you own a Harley-Davidson T-shirt, Verne made it), Dick Day (can't for the life of me imagine why he puts up with me!), Ben Campbell (a.k.a. Santa Claus), Leigh Dorrington (of the Pendine Racing Group), Bill DeArment (if you own a Channellock too, Bill made it), Ted Metzger (if you've ever used an I&T Shop Guide, Ted made it), Allen Petersen (if you own a Vise-Grip tool . . .), Jim Cossaart (a dentist–windmill repairman–auto racing buff . . . Well, you get the idea). I appreciate all the help, tools, information, guidance, and cooperation I have gotten from you friends. Thank you.

I owe thanks too to Michael Dregni at Voyageur Press. He has been in my corner a long time, often when it didn't appear that there would be a lot of business opportunities for us as a team. Nonetheless, Michael stuck with it. His books are beautiful as well as useful. And Michael was the one who came up with the plan for this anthology of my *Successful Farming* columns, convinced Meredith, *Successful Farming*, and me that it would work, jumped through all the hoops, pushed all the buttons, and opened all the doors to bring the idea to realization—and print. We all owe him thanks. I know I sure do.

Finally, I want to thank my mom, Bertha Welsch. I am still learning what a grand soul she is, and every new thing I learn makes me love her more. It may seem strange to you (it will to her!) that I even mention her name in this book—including in a tractor book a woman who has never sat on a tractor, maybe never even touched one, who doesn't know a torque wrench from a foot-pound. In fact, it's stranger than you can possibly know. She read only a few pages from one of my recent books before tightly closing it and putting it away. She told me firmly that books should educate and enlighten, and any book that uses the "f-word," as this one did, clearly could not meet those criteria. Once she reached that word—"fart," for those of you who may be thinking wrongly about how my mom sees this world—she had had enough. Mom, I hope you *will* like this one. It was you, Mom, who gave me a love for learning, and books, and words, and wit, and humor.

Chapter 1

Roger's Rules for Collecting Old Iron

There's more to collecting and restoring old tractors than nuts and bolts. A lot more. In fact, nuts and bolts are the least of it. Ask our marriage counselor. Don't get me wrong: Lovely Linda is a wonderful wife and friend and she has endured more than any one woman should have to put up with. I'm the first to admit that life with me isn't easy. I admit that, even though I don't always believe it.

Things got tense when I began collecting Allis-Chalmers WC tractors. I had one WC for almost twenty years before it occurred to me that it might be nice to have two. And once I had two, I thought it would really be handy to have a couple of junked WCs around for parts, and along with the parts tractors I got a couple of "runners." So then there were six. And I got a good deal on one that had been sitting in a shed for nearly twenty-five years, and I think I have another couple lined up not far from here, if I can just work out the details.

It has taken the better part of two years, but just last week Lovely Linda finally sighed, "I give up. I've lost track. I have no idea how many tractors you have." It was a moment of triumph—but it was not without, as they say, its downside.

I first realized I was getting into trouble when I overheard Lovely Linda telling her mother, "It used to be that he'd go to bed, smiling and sighing. I'd look over and see that he was reading a *Playboy* magazine. Now when he's smiling and sighing, it's because he's thumbing through an Allis-Chalmers parts catalog!"

Over the past couple years, I have collected advice along with my WCs, and I think it is only neighborly that I pass along to you what I have learned. If you're married and are thinking about getting into the old iron business, forget trivial things like socket wrenches and bearing pullers and lay the groundwork for your new hobby by carefully studying the following rules, Roger's Rules for Collecting Old Iron!

Rule #1: Collect only one model and make of tractor—nothing but John Deere Bs or Allis-Chalmers Gs, for example. When all your tractors are the same color and shape, it's harder, if not impossible, for anyone (if you catch my drift) to figure out how many tractors you actually have.

Rule #2: Similarly, never line up your tractors, ever. Nothing distresses a difficult spouse more than seeing twelve old tractors lined up, looking for all the world like a burning pile of hundred-dollar bills. Scatter the tractors around—a couple behind the shed, one or two in the shed, another beside the garage—so that it's not possible for anyone (if you know who I mean) to see more than two or three from any one perspective. Your hobby will be less "irritating" that way.

Rule #3: For pretty much the same reason, don't number your tractors. Give them names. You'd be surprised how much less trouble you will have if you talk about "Steel Wheels" or "Sweet Allis" rather than "Allis-Chalmers WC #14."

Rule #4: Early in your collecting, buy a tractor you don't want. Sell it again as quickly as you can; don't worry about making money on the transaction. The main thing is to get a tractor and get rid of it. Then, for years, you can say, "Yes, Angel Face, I do have six John Deere Bs, and they are in the shed while our car is out in the weather, but that doesn't mean that I will always have six John Deere Bs. *Remember the one I got rid of a few years ago? I'm thinking of selling another one any day now so we can put the car in the garage.*"

If you have a friend who collects tractors, make arrangements for him to drop off a tractor now and again. That way you can say (if anyone asks) that you bought it. Then have it hauled off again, and say you sold it. With this system, you will re-establish your reputation for moderation every couple of years or so.

Warning: About the time I accumulated my sixth or seventh Allis WC I thought I'd be smart, so I bought a lovely little Allis C. Linda and our nine-year-old daughter Antonia were in the farmyard as I unloaded this lovely little item that needed only some wheel work and a new wiring harness.

"I see you bought yourself another tractor that doesn't run," said Linda.

"Guess what, dear?" I beamed. "I didn't buy myself another Allis-Chalmers. I bought *you* an Allis-Chalmers! She's yours, and ain't she cute?"

I could tell by the look on her face that she was about as excited as she was the Christmas I gave her a new drain cleaner attachment for her vacuum sweeper, but I wasn't at all prepared for what she said next: "How much can I get for it?"

"Er, uh, I didn't get it for you to sell, Honey Cakes. I was thinking, if you don't want to drive it all the time, I can take it into town now and then just to keep the oil stirred up for you. It won't be any trouble at all."

"Well, thanks, Rog, you're really too sweet. I don't deserve a darling like you. How much can I get for it?"

I almost broke into tears at the thought of someone loading that great tractor onto a trailer and driving off with it. I was thinking that I should have gone with my first impulse and said that it had followed me home and asked if I could maybe keep it, but thank goodness, about that time my mind kicked into road gear. "Actually, I thought that if you wouldn't mind sharing, it could also be Antonia's tractor. Right. That's it! Eventually it'll be Antonia's tractor."

Antonia leaped into the C's seat with a squeal and started twisting the steering wheel and making tractor noises. Linda snorted something about me fixing my own supper that night—that is, if I was intending to stay over—and headed back toward the house while I helped Antonia bond with her lovely new tractor. That was a close call, and my advice to you is not to buy your wife a tractor. In fact, you're better off sticking with the idea of the drain cleaner attachment for the vacuum sweeper.

Rule #5: Pay for tractors with a cashier's check, postal money order, or cash. These leave far less evidence than checks drawn on the family account. Once you have gotten possession of a tractor and paid for it, *eat the stubs, carbon copies, or receipts immediately.* Such things have a way of becoming an embarrassment later. Take it from me.

Some collectors like to point out to skeptical marriage partners that what with interest rates so low these days, buying old tractors is actually an investment, a way of being sure the spouse will be "taken care of and comfortable should something . . . something terrible happen." Doesn't work with Lovely Linda. She thinks Allis-Chalmers WCs *are* the "something terrible."

Rule #6: Now and then, buy a wreck "for parts," even if you don't need the parts, even if it has no salvageable parts. In fact, you might consider hauling an extra wreck or two whenever you haul home a good machine, if possible, on the same trailer or truck. This is called "liability averaging."

If your spouse says something about it being strange that you have money for yet another tractor but not enough for a new refrigerator, point indignantly to the tractors on the trailer: the beautiful one on steel and in running condition for which you paid $1,600, and the two rusted hulks you got for $50 each. Then huff (or whine, depending on what has worked in the past), "Snookums, I got those for a little more than $500 each and the one in the back is easily worth $2,000 just as it stands. That's a tidy profit of $400—*which is more than four times what I paid for the other two*." See? Doesn't that make you sound like an investment wizard?

Some collectors find it effective to add something like, "It's pretty hard to find a good refrigerator for $500!" But it has been my experience that a smart-aleck attitude can fairly directly lead to the purchase of a $500 refrigerator.

Rule #7: When things get critical in the household, consider dragging home a tractor without a transmission or rear wheels. If there is complaint, you say something like, "Tractor? What tractor? That's not a tractor! That's only a front end. Not even close to a tractor." Then, a couple weeks later, bring home a rear end, minus the radiator, engine, and front wheels. "What tractor?" you say. "That's no tractor! That's only a rear end. Not even close to a tractor." Don't try this, however, more than once every couple years.

Rule #8: Have an implement dealer, salvage yard proprietor, or friend call you now and then when you're not at home and tell your spouse, "Rog told me to keep an eye on the Allis WC going at the auction up at Centerville Saturday, but it sold for $1,200 and I know there's no way a financially cautious and responsible guy like Rog would pay that much for a tractor so I didn't even make a bid on it for him."

Not only will this make you look real good, but the next time you do buy a tractor, say something like, "Lovie-Bear, this beauty only cost me $300, which means we're $900 ahead of where we would have been if I'd gotten the one that came up for sale at Centerville. Why, if I keep saving money like this, we'll be able to go on a Caribbean cruise next winter." If you say it fast enough, it might work.

Rule #9: If your mate insults your tractor work by referring to it as "rustoration" or "tinkering," laugh a lighthearted laugh that makes it clear that tractors are not to you what shoes are to Imelda Marcos. Remind her that you could sell all your tools and tractors any time you want and that you really resent her slipping those twelve-step program brochures under your pillow every night.

Rule #10: Your situation may deteriorate to the point where your mate asks, "What do you love more, me or your blasted tractors?" Whatever you do, don't ask for time to think it over.

I have tried to couch the above information in nonsexist language. Yes, I am dealing with my wife Linda—and what a darling she is! But there is every indication that my daughter Antonia is going to be a tractor nut like her Old Man and will be using these same devices to smooth things over with her husband.

The above suggestions are not dishonest or deceptive, exactly. They are ways to make life easier for your spouse. In fact, now that I think about it, these little acts of diplomacy are actually a kindness, a way to smooth the road for someone you love. Following Roger's Rules is a way of being a better person. People who follow Roger's Rules are *good* people. In fact, I feel so good about myself, I think I'll go out and buy myself another tractor! It'll be a good investment. I'll have it hauled in at night. That way I won't bother Lovely Linda.

Chapter 2

Roger's Rules
for Restoring a Tractor
for Fun and Profit

I have been in this business of restoring old tractors for, oh, almost a whole year now, so I pretty much know everything there is to know. And I am fully prepared to share all that information. No sense in us both making the same mistakes.

The most important, most frequently asked question about tractor restoration is, "Why?" (Or, in the case of my wife Lovely Linda, "WHY?!!!") My own reasons range from cosmetic (I find that after a day lying under a tractor, putting on an oil pan maybe, my hair takes on new body and luster) to philosophical (uh . . .).

I started working on Allis-Chalmers WCs last summer. I'd just come off a week with my CBS News crew, right after a week on book tour for Random House. Then, after spending one full hour alone with my chatty, curious six-year-old daughter Antonia—the series of stresses on my nervous system pushed my blood pressure to something like 489-over-366, whatever that means.

I say "something like . . ." because our blood-pressure gauge peaked out around the 300-mark and started making little fire alarm sounds. My pulse sounded like the firing of an AK-47 automatic assault rifle.

At that moment, I decided I would spend the next day away from the telephone and my office, away from the mail basket, away from anyone from New York City, away from everything that means anything. I'll . . . I'll . . . I've got it! I'll repair the broken brake on my Allis WC!

Now, you have to understand that up to this point in my life I had never so much as changed the oil in a vehicle. I hate vehicles. Like everyone else in America, I rely on vehicles, and I hate being that dependent on anything or anyone. I had no interest in new tractors, let alone old ones. My 1937 Allis WC was simply a utility tractor to me—a tool. But I spent the next day in a gentle, warm sun, taking the brake lever and shoe out of a junked tractor and putting them on my Allis.

No Hurry, No Schedule

I wasn't in a hurry because my Allis was essentially only a backup, my International 300 being the real farm workhorse. The Allis had worked just fine with one brake for fifteen years, so it didn't really matter if I repaired it or not. And there wasn't any sort of schedule, so if I didn't finish it that day, so what? No pressures, no problems.

That evening my blood pressure was 4.5-over-2. My pulse was about two a minute. I decided that anything that had that sort of calming influence over my much-abused body deserved further exploration. And thus I became a dedicated tractor tinkerer.

Why tractors? Because you can work on them standing up, for one thing, and for a guy of my age and build, that's really important.

Why *old* tractors? Because there's none of that foreign metric nonsense with old tractors, just good ol' American inches, pounds, hairs, and smidgins.

In fact, with old tractors there aren't even problems with all that electrical stuff like amps and volts that nobody understands anyway. On an Allis WC there are exactly four wires, one leading to each spark plug. Occasionally, even that can be confusing for a guy like me, but four wires is within my grasp. Most of the time. I think.

With old tractors, you don't hook up a computer to figure out what is going on inside. One of my ancient Allis-Chalmers manuals shows how to brace up a tree limb so you can pull the engine on your

19-horsepower beast. The manufacturer understood that these machines were going to be worked on out under a cottonwood tree by a guy who owned three wrenches, a claw hammer, and a bent screwdriver—which is to say, me.

Your Own Personal NAPA Store

Of course, while you don't *need* a lot of tools, a big part of restoring old tractors is buying tools. There's not a man alive, and only a few women, who wouldn't be perfectly happy buying a NAPA store or Snap-On truck, closing its doors to the public, and spending a lifetime admiring and inventorying all those neat, shiny tools. Having a "shop" for restoring tractors is a lot like owning a NAPA or Snap-On franchise. Except without all the trouble of customers.

In fact, tractor restoration is a great economic alternative for those times when your $500,000 in certificates of deposit or gold bullion just isn't paying off the way you think it should.

Say you buy a junked John Deere B for $500, haul it into your $5,000 shop, and use your $2,000 worth of tools to take it apart and start repairs. You put about $2,500 worth of parts into it and a few hundred dollars worth of liquids and gooey things. You invest a couple thousand hours of labor and a few thousand dollars for medical treatment (burns, busted knuckles, stomach pumping for the time you poured the Mountain Dew on a stuck tappet and drank the Liquid Wrench), and before you know it, you have transformed a $500 piece of green junk into a $1,200 showpiece, thus more than doubling your initial investment. Where else can you get that kind of return on your buck? Isn't America great?!

A remarkable proportion of time spent on restoration consists of sitting or standing around and staring. Take auction sales, for example.

That's where you get old tractors. Well, not exactly. It's not where *you* get old tractors, it's where other people get old tractors. See, you can go to all the sales you want, but you will never buy a tractor. They always go too high. Always.

If you take $300 to Fleischblum's sale, the tractor you had your eye on there will go for $310. If you take $350 to Kosmolinski's sale, their tractor will go for $360.

On the other hand, the next time you talk with your buddy Lunchbox, he'll say, "Kosmolinski's? You shoulda been at the sale over at Grembeck's. His WC, never spent a night out of the shed, went for $35, with a spare set of wheels."

The thing to do is to tell Lunchbox that the next time he sees a WC going for less than $300, he should pick it up for you. He will, but funny thing, it will always cost you exactly $300. He's bidding on a tractor for you at Freeble's auction where WCs are going for $300 while you stand in Widow Dinkster's farmyard and stare as her WC goes for $8,222. I don't know why. That's just the way it works.

When you're not standing and staring at auction sales, you'll be standing and staring at parts stores. ("Now, was that a $9/32$-inch bolt $33/8$ inches long, or a $3/92$-inch bolt 32 inches long?") Or at tractor manuals ("insufficient clearance shims in the crush shell will result in spontaneous destruction of the engine within the first minute of operation, so torque all castellated nuts to 22.2 square foot-pounds on $1/4$-inch lugs, 47.3 inch-ounces on $37/64$-inch lugs, or else"). And finally, you'll be staring at your wife. ("What do you mean, what will I do with it if I ever get it running?")

Forty-Six Parts, More or Less

Old tractors are good tractors because they have only forty-six parts. Okay, some tractors have a few more, some a few less, but forty-six parts is a good working number. The frame of an Allis WC is two 9-foot-long pieces of angle iron with some holes in them. And that's it. So, I can understand the frame on an Allis WC. I not only understand a WC's water pump, I can *find* a WC's water pump. Try that in your BMW.

This past winter I completely dismantled an Allis WC, touching all forty-six parts in it. And I put it back together. No, it still doesn't run, but at this point in my restoration career, "running" is not the most important thing in the world.

By the way, I have made a general announcement that should that WC ever decide to go ahead and run, I am going to drive it up to town and park it right outside the door of Eric's Tavern. I'm going to pull a big table over close to the door and prop the door open so I can hear it run. Then I'm going to invite everyone in town to join me in a glass of cheap champagne. Eric thinks it's a great idea, but says that he isn't going to order the champagne yet because the stuff he carries only has a shelf life of three years.

Everyone's a comedian, but not everyone is a tractor restoration expert.

Chapter 3

Roger's Simple Guide to Carburator Adjustment

Mel Grim up at the Sinclair station isn't afraid of anything—he'll take on any automotive task. At least that's what I used to think. And then I asked him to work on a carburetor.

"I don't do carburetors," he said, obviously embarrassed.

"Why don't you do carburetors?"

"Just don't," he replied.

"Why not?" I wondered again.

"Don't," he blurted.

Turns out, Mel is afraid of carburetors. That's okay, because so is almost everyone else. One of the things that has surprised me as I've learned ever more about tractor repair and restoration is how timid everyone is about carburetors. Well, I'm not afraid of carburetors. And by the time I get through with you, you won't be afraid of carburetors either.

It's as simple as this: a carburetor mixes air and fuel. It has two little adjusting screws: one is for adjusting the fuel-air mixture when the engine is idling, the other is for adjusting the engine when it's running at full power. Anyone who knows anything about engines and carburetors will be able to tell you which is which on your particular model, although you'll probably be able to figure it out for yourself just by turning the needles a little in each direction while the machine is running.

Let's take a look at this carburetor on one of my Allis WCs. Hand me that screwdriver. While the engine is at idle, I'll fiddle with this screw until the tractor runs smoothly. Then, while the engine is running at good speed, I dink around with the other screw until the engine runs well there, and that's pretty much all you need to know about carburetor adjustment. The job is done. Does that sound like the kind of thing that strikes terror into the hearts of strong men?

Whoops.

I guess we must have shaken something loose because you'll note that a little drop of gas has formed on the bottom of the carburetor casting. Easy enough. Just tighten this little nut the idle adjustment screw goes through and . . . well, as luck would have it, that appears to make the leak a little worse.

Let's shut off the engine and take a look at this. It's no big deal, believe me. We'll have this problem taken care of in a jiffy.

We'll need to take the carburetor off, because I think the float needs adjustment, which is what is giving us that gas drip. No problem. Simply remove the two nuts holding the carburetor to the bottom of the manifold.

Whoops.

Hey, breaking off a bolt like that is a standard part of tractor work, believe me. We'll get back to that in a minute, but in the meantime, let's take a look at what's going on inside the carburetor.

Whoa!

Did you see that little spring fly out of there? Never saw that before. It must have been the culprit. Probably wasn't holding the float right or something. It went over in this direction, can't have gone far.

Ouch!

The spring must have been a little on the tired side to flatten out like that when I hardly even stepped on it with my full weight. Well,

Mel will probably have one something like it in his spare parts box. We can check tomorrow when we go to town for a carburetor gasket.

Until then, let's take a look at that broken manifold bolt. Drilling it out and replacing it requires removal of the entire manifold, which is no more complicated that it appears. The manifold is held onto the engine block by eight studs with brass nuts. Take the nuts off and the manifold comes right off.

Whoops. Whoops.

Whoops again.

Don't worry about that. I've never seen anyone take a manifold off without breaking a stud or two. Or three. All you do is drill a little hole precisely in the center, take an EZ-Out or any of the dozens of similar extraction devices, screw it backwards into the little hole, and turn firmly with a wrench. Here, I'll show you the process.

Whoops.

We've broken off the extractor in the hole, a bit more of a problem since an extractor has the hardness of a banker's heart and you're not going to drill it out with whatever you have. We'll have to get that engine uptown somehow and have a mechanic blow it out with a cutting torch. Trust me—it'll only take a few minutes. Help me drag out this engine hoist and we'll start to pull the engine off the transmission.

What are the rods inside the holes from the manifold, you ask? Those are valve stems. Why are they all covered with oil and crud? Hmmm. It looks like we're going to have to remove the head and work on those valves.

We'll have to take off the water pump before we can get to the head, as you can plainly see. The water pump is the thing with the fan blades on it. Just three bolts to take off and it'll be free. And I guess to get the pump off this tractor, you also have to remove the radiator.

Whoops.

Don't worry about that. We can get it fixed later. But in the meanwhile, look at this! Whoever worked on this tractor last stopped up a leaky pan gasket with window putty. Real bright guy. See, it comes right off! And look at the oil run out. Yuk. If you're going to do something, might just as well do it right, so we'll drop the pan and put a new gasket on. And to do that, looks like we have to take off the steering shaft.

Whoops.

Ouch.

I don't think that's going to need stitches, is it? Happens all the time. See right there, on my left hand? Same kind of thing. Almost took the entire finger off on that one. Pretty much healed up good as new. Except I can't play the banjo any more. Well . . .

Maybe we'll have better luck with the oil pan. Hand me that speed wrench and ratchet.

Whoops.

Well, since we have to take the block up to a mechanic anyway, it won't be any more of a problem to have him take out the broken pan and water pump bolts too. See how everything is starting to dovetail here? Falling together like a jigsaw puzzle . . .

Well, no, the pistons shouldn't shake around in there like that, and now that you mention it, neither should the front wheels and the drive shaft. We'll have plenty of time because we're going to have to order a full set of gaskets anyway, which sometimes takes a few weeks, so we might just as well do this job right.

And isn't that just the way it goes? If we had *tried* to get a little washer like that to fall through that tiny hole into the water jacket, it would have taken us hours. Maybe while the mechanic is working on the broken studs, he can fish the washer out of the block with a magnet, or something.

What the heck, while we're at it, let's take a look at the clutch, transmission, and final drive. Complicated? Nah. You'll run into a lot of guys who are afraid of tearing into a transmission or final drive. All they can talk about is how difficult it is to deal with bull gears, the great big hunks of iron at the back wheels. Bull gears are simple mechanical devices just like everything else on this tractor: if you use common sense and patience, and buy your Liquid Wrench in 60-gallon drums, none of this is impossible.

All you have to do to get to the bull gears is remove the wheels, which are held on by another set of studs—these threaded rods. The ones you see right here.

Whoops.

Boy, that's liable to be a little tough getting back in there, don't you think?

Whoops.

Ouch.

Did you see where that clip went?

Whoops.

There it is. Okay, no problem. That should heal up by next week, and I'm right-handed anyway, and that hand was going to need some attention when we go back to the house anyway.

Maybe while we clean up the mess (any good solvent will handle both blood and gear grease or, as is more common, a blend of the two), we can take another look at that carburetor.

Whoops.

Chapter 4

Ask Mr. Rustoration Answer Man, Part I

I have received a lot of questions from readers about collecting and restoring old tractors. Okay, most of the questions—and the toughest ones, I'll have to admit—have come from my wife, Lovely Linda, but I have also gotten a few from other collectors and restorers. (With, I might note, a lot nicer language than Linda uses these days when I drag home yet another battered Allis-Chalmers tractor. Where did she learn language like that?)

As Mrs. Gronie, your high school English teacher, used to tell you, "If you have a question, go ahead and ask it because you can be sure that there are other of your friends and classmates who have the same question." In the spirit of Mrs. Gronie's presumption of universal bewilderment, I hereby share some of our readers' questions and my responses with you.

Dear Mr. Rustoration Answer Man:

I'm a beginner in the complicated world of mechanicking, so there are a lot of things I still don't know about restoring old tractors. For example, after a day in the shop, my hands are black with dirt and grease, and I haven't found a way to get the stuff off. Days later, even after my knuckles have healed, my fingernails are still ringed with the black grunge.

Drecky in Denver

Dear Drecky:

I'm not sure I understand your problem. I haven't had this sort of trouble since I started stirring my coffee with my fingers.

Dear Mr. Rustoration Answer Man:

Yesterday I was working on a carburetor and dropped a tiny little brass screw. I heard it hit the floor and roll, so I had a rough idea what direction it took, but I could not for the life of me find the blasted thing. It is impossible to buy a replacement. *I must find that screw!* Can you help me, Mr. Rustoration Answer Man?

Frustrated in Philadelphia

Dear Frustrated:

You bet I can help you! The first thing experienced mechanics like me do in a situation like this is to try to think like the lost part: Where would you go if you were an unappreciated brass carburetor screw and you wanted to make the most of this, your moment in the spotlight? Which is to say, the experienced mechanic assumes the worst: He immediately goes to the most remote corner of the shop, back behind a pile of filthy, rusted manifolds with razor-sharp edges, filled with mouse nests. Two hours later, covered with dirt, grease, and blood, he reaches the distant, dark corner behind the manifolds and finds— nothing.

The lost screw has outmaneuvered the mechanic once again. The thing is, that little brass screw knows you are going to look first in the most unlikely place, i.e., the most likely place. The brass screw will, therefore, be in neither place. And that's the heart of the matter.

The lost part will never be where you look for it *first*. Ask anyone. Review your own experience. The lost part will always be in the *last* place you look. (But you can't start at the last place, because then it becomes the first place).

What you have to do is to go ahead and perform your search, even though you now know it won't do you any good. It's like trying to use reason while arguing with your spouse: of course it won't do any good, but there is something within you that simply drives you to do it.

You *must* look in the remote, dirty corner under the manifolds, even though the part isn't there, because, well, just because. In fact, you'll have to look everywhere in the shop, under everything, behind everything, not finding the part, until you're finally so frustrated, you throw a wrench through the window, stomp out of the shop, track grease across your wife's freshly mopped kitchen floor, and mix yourself a stiff drink.

Later that evening you'll find your lost part in the bib pocket of your overalls.

Dear Mr. Rustoration Answer Man:

I have a pretty good mechanical sense but I can't figure out electrical devices like magnetos. How does a magneto work, Mr. Rustoration Answer Man?

Curious in Columbus

Dear Curious:

Magic.

Dear Mr. Rustoration Answer Man:

I put together a real nice shop for working on old iron and I have spent many pleasurable hours out there. The problem is, my friends keep borrowing my tools. So, every time I need a ½-inch-drive socket ratchet, it's off somewhere halfway across the county. What's to do, Mr. Rustoration Answer Man?

Looted in St. Louis

Dear Looted:

This is an easy one: get yourself a new set of tools. Then get yourself a new set of friends.

The problem is a lot tougher, of course, when the borrower is your own kid. My pal Slick and I were discussing this dilemma not a week ago. His son had dropped by and helped himself to a car trunk full of tools just about the same time my kid Chris pulled the same stunt.

Slick is a real philosopher, and I think he hit the bull's-eye when he shook his head and lamented, "You know, Rog, it's a real shame when our own boys come rolling into our shops and help themselves to our tools, whisking away in a matter of minutes what it took us years to filch from our fathers."

"Shame" isn't strong enough a word for it, Slick.

Dear Mr. Rustoration Answer Man:

I am trying to remove a pinion gear from the steering pedestal of my tractor. I was darn near smug about the problem because my wife gave me a three-arm gear puller for Christmas, so for once I was ready with the right tool for exactly this situation. I read the directions for the puller carefully and set about installing the puller on the gear. Hours later I was still trying to wrestle the puller arms in place, get the puller shaft centered, tighten the puller nut, and apply pressure on the gear all at the same time.

Mr. Rustoration Answer Man, it seems obvious to me after struggling with this thing for the better part of a day that the only way I'll ever be able to use a three-arm gear puller is if I grow another hand.

Baffled in Buffalo

Dear Baffled:

Yes.

Dear Mr. Rustoration Answer Man:

I cannot for the life of me figure out the size of the set bolts that hold the shifter forks on the transmission shafts of my 1937 Allis-Chalmers WC. The square head of the bolt is ever-so slightly too big for $\%_{64}$-inch wrench, ever-so slightly too small for a $\frac{5}{32}$-inch ($\frac{10}{64}$-inch) wrench. I took the shifter to a top-notch, fully equipped machinist and he said that he can't figure it out either. He can't even make a $\frac{19}{128}$-inch wrench, precisely between $\frac{9}{64}$-inch and $\frac{10}{64}$-inch, fit the bolt head. So what's the deal?

Misfit in Minneapolis

Dear Misfit:

I'm glad you asked this question because I am one of the few guys around who can answer it. Bohumil Brzd, Allis design engineer from 1925 until 1942, chose this charming way to pay homage to his beloved homeland, the Republic of Irregula (absorbed by Metricia shortly after the First World War). The size of the bolt head is, as you correctly note, nonexistent in the modern world. It persists however as the Irregulian Pft, based on half the width of a gnat's gluteus maximus. Your only option is to go at that set-bolt with an 18-inch pipe wrench. (I know there's no room in the shifter housing for an 18-inch pipe wrench, but then that wasn't your question, now, was it?)

Dear Mr. Rustoration Answer Man:

I have been working on old tractors for about five years. I've read everything you write about the subject and follow your advice as closely as I can, so I trust your judgment. Lately I've noticed that my coffee tastes like Liquid Wrench. What's going on?

Yucky in Yuma

Dear Yucky:

Beats me.

Well, there you have it—a wealth of information garnered from many long years of experience. Now all I have to do is come up with some answers for Lovely Linda.

Chapter 5

Ask Mr. Rustoration Answer Man, Part II: Restorer, Mechanic, Gearhead, Enthusiast, Tinkerer, or Dabbler?

Most of the time, we don't have much doubt about what we are. In fact, far more than we might like, people are frequently way too eager to tell us what we are. "You blooming idiot, what do you think you are, a race car driver?" See, that's pretty clear, isn't it? You may or may not be a race car driver, but there's not much question about being a blooming idiot.

The situation is not all that clear, however, when you work on old tractors. I know I'm not in the class of those who *restore* tractors so they're better looking and running better than they were when they came off the assembly line. But I also know I've come a long way from where I was when I first twisted off a manifold lug and figured I'd ruined the engine.

Well, you know by now you can count on me to give important issues like this a lot of serious thought and to share the results with you. There's no longer a need for you to stand there scratching your head when someone asks you what it is, exactly, that you do with old tractors. Take the following handy test in the privacy of your own shop and you will know exactly where you stand in the world of tractor rustoration—restorer, mechanic, gearhead, enthusiast, tinkerer, or dabbler.

Answer each of the following questions and circle the score of your response (the number to the right). At the end of the exam, total your score, consult the scoring guide, and you will never again have to wonder what you are. And if this test doesn't make it perfectly clear what you are, I'll bet your wife will be glad to tell you—any time you have the courage to ask.

Question   Points

A. You know:

The color of your tractor	1
The make of your tractor	2
The year of your tractor	3
The serial number of your tractor	4
The tolerances of your tractor's rod bearings	5
Your tractor's religious orientation	6

B. You want:

A shiny new tractor	1
To sell your tractor	2
To keep your tractor	3
To fix your tractor	4
To restore your tractor	5
A meaningful relationship with your tractor	6

C. You:

Used to have a wrench here somewhere	1
Borrow a wrench when needed	2
Have a wrench	3
Own a wrench	4
Have a full set of sockets, 6- and 8-point	5
Are on a first-name basis with the entire Sears tool department	6

D. You:

Have a wife who complains you never fix anything	1
Have a wife who complains you never fix anything important	2
Have a wife who complains	3
Have a girlfriend who complains	4
Once met a girl but she had the wrong kind of tractor	5
Used to have a wife around here somewhere	6

E. You have grease:

On your handkerchief	1
On your shirt cuff	2
On your nose	3
Under your fingernails	4
Under your toenails	5
Where the sun don't shine	6

F. You do your shop work:

By watching a mechanic change your tractor's oil	1
In the driveway	2
Under a shade tree	3
In your car's garage	4
In your tractor shop	5
In your kitchen	6

G. Your tractor is:

Around here somewhere	1
Parked under a mulberry tree	2
Under a tarp behind the barn	3
In a shed	4
Locked in the shop	5
In a Swiss bank	6

H. You call your tractor:

It	1
The tractor	2
By its manufacturer's name	3
He	4
She	5
Snookums-Bear Sweetie-Muffin	6

I. Last year your tractor restoration expenses were:

$0	1
$50	2
$500	3
Can't say	4
Won't say	5
Still in litigation	6

J. You:

Were left your tractor in Grandpa's will	1
Were given it for a lawn decoration	2
Accidentally got it at an auction when you scratched your nose	3
Actually bought it on purpose	4
Paid for it while your wife looked on	5
Traded one of your children for it	6

Total of Points from All Questions

There is a potential of 60 possible points. Add up all your points and then match your score with the ratings schedule below:

56–60 points = Restorer First Class: Take a look at the Yellow Pages under "Psychiatrists, Emergency Care," and do it soon.

51–55 points = Restorer: Try not to breathe any more parts solvent fumes, okay?

46–50 points = Master Mechanic: Roosevelt, you say? No, we've had several presidents since then.

41–45 points = Mechanic: Rumelys? No, they don't make them anymore.

36–40 points = Gearhead: Get your wrench away from that Allis.

31–35 points = Gearhead Junior: No, I don't want to sell my tractor.

26–30 points = Enthusiast: You need a carburetor? And you say money's no object? I think we can work together on this.

21–25 points = Enthusiast Second Grade: Have you seen the new Kamikazi S12 tractor? It's real shiny. And cute.

16–20 points = Tinkerer: You wouldn't take $100 for that pile of rust, would you?

11–15 points = Apprentice Tinkerer: Tell you what, buddy, just 'cause I like your looks, I'll haul that junk outta here for you.

6–10 points = Dabbler: Tell you what, buddy, just 'cause I like your looks, I'll haul that junker Cletrac outa here for you. For $50.

0–5 points = Beginning Dabbler: You know what you need? You need a good tractor. A real classic. And I have just the one for you. Step over here to this shed with me and I'm going to make you the investment opportunity of your life, young man. What you see here is a rare prize of a tractor, and just because I like your looks . . .

Chapter 6

Ask Mr. Rustoration Answer Man, Part III

In my continuing effort to bring the latest information to light, I have once again assembled the most challenging questions sent to me at Rustoration HQ here in Dannebrog over the past few months. I've researched the answers and now I'm going to pass them along to you for your enjoyment and education. No, no, don't bother to thank me. It's just part of being—ta-da!—Mr. Rustoration Answer Man!

Dear Mr. Rustoration Answer Man:

I am about to get into tractor restoration. What are the most expensive parts I will have to buy in rebuilding an antique tractor?

Curious in California

Dear Curious:

I presume you are not thinking of body parts, right?

The most expensive part for a tractor repair is always whatever part you happen to need. If you buy seven junk tractors for parts, the first time you need an oil pressure valve assembly, you will find that all seven of those tractors are missing the oil pressure valve assembly. Or whatever other part you need. Brake lever, timing gear, water pump—doesn't matter. Whatever you need, you won't have, you will have a hard time finding, and will turn out to be made out of Exploitium, the most valuable material known to man.

My theory is that when farm boys in 1953 needed fishing sinkers, for some reason they all removed exactly the same part from every tractor of any particular make; every Allis WC carb, every Avery oil cup, every John Deere B battery cover, etc. I don't know why, but I consider it proof that there's divine order in the universe.

Dear Mr. Rustoration Answer Man:

Our local mechanic says that if I'm going to get into tractor mechanicking, the first thing I need to do is lay in a good supply of "ferrous monofilament utility connector." What is that?

Bewildered in Beloit

Dear Bewildered:

Baling wire. And don't skimp on the duct tape either.

Dear Mr. Rustoration Answer Man:

I have a bunch of old Allis WC parts, like carbs, mags, iron wheels, cast-iron oil pans, belt pulleys, water pumps, that sort of thing. I have no idea what they're worth, if anything. What do you suggest I do?

Cluttered in Cleveland

Dear Cluttered:

Uh, you're absolutely right, of course. The parts you mention are utterly worthless. Tell you what: if you ship them along to good ol' Mr. Rustoration Answer Man, you can count on me to see that the useless parts are appropriately recycled in such a way that they will do the most good while causing the least harm. Yessir, that's me—when they don't call me Mr. Rustoration Answer Man, they call me Mr. Helpful.

Dear Mr. Rustoration Answer Man:

I took apart the fuel system of an old tractor I picked up for next to nothing and am now trying to restore. Whenever I shake the gas tank, there are funny clunks and rattles from its innards. What do you think?

Baffled in Buffalo

Dear Baffled:

First, I think it takes a lot of gall to ask me a real question. Second, I think it's great that it's a question I can actually answer.

I have found walnut shells in old gas tanks (put there by a squirrel, probably) and peanuts (moved there right in my shop by an ambitious mouse). I have shaken remnants of gas caps, a bitters bottle, various bolts and nuts, two screwdrivers, ladies underwear (must have been quite a story there!), and several mouse skeletons from old gas tanks.

When I first started working on my Allises, I had the good fortune to attend a restoration seminar taught by the Grand Master, Oppie Gravert, who is now in tractor heaven, if anyone is. He told his assembled audience a few dumb-stuff-found-in-old-gas-tank stories and concluded that in fact he had rarely worked on a tank that didn't include a couple of wayward "gas gauges."

I was mystified. None of my tractors—not one of them—has anything remotely like a gas gauge. Are Allis WCs the only tractors without gas gauges? Had I somehow missed a little dial tucked away back behind the tank somewhere? How could I have not seen something as obvious as a gas gauge?

So, Rog the Professor holds up his hand and asks, "Mr. Gravert, what do you mean, 'gas gauge?'"

Oppie, of course, held up a stick. Professor Rog crawled under his chair and pretended to go to sleep.

And by the by, when welding on a gas tank, be sure to sit on it so it doesn't get away from you in the event of a backfire—a trick I learned so long ago from my favorite uncle, the late Barney Flapdoodle, who now enjoys his eternal rest in Omaha. And Lincoln. And Des Moines.

Dear Mr. Rustoration Answer Man:

My wife, Dorothy, thought it was kind of neat when I brought home my first old tractor and bought a set of Made-in-Taiwan wrenches for $11 so I could work on it under the cottonwood tree in our backyard.

A couple months later she seemed a trifle miffed when I came home with another tractor, a rolling, sixty-two-drawer mechanic's cabinet full of Craftsman tools, and hired my brother-in-law to build a small shop for me. She got downright testy by the time I came home with tractor number twelve, received my Customer-of-the-Month Award from Sears, and finished building my state-of-the-art welding shop. Last week, when I dragged in the twenty-ninth tractor, upgraded to Snap-Ons, and moved my repair work into the house and the family out to the old shop, she filed divorce papers. Can you explain women to me, Mr. Rustoration Answer Man?

Ousted in Ogallala

Dear Ousted:

I know people who can explain differentials, magnetos, and magnafluxing but they can't explain women. But I do know something about the laws of nature, and your question deals with one of them. Sir Isaac Newton, when he was not inventing gravity and fig bars, came up with something called the Third Law of Thermodynamics. It says something to the effect that energy is turned into heat, and heat is turned into energy, and dust returns to dust, and never the twain shall meet, but nothing is ever really "lost" in the process.

I have done a little fine-tuning on Newton's theories. It was me, for example, who figured out that calories are never lost either. Whatever weight a skinny girl in Denver loses, travels by micron waves and sticks to some fat guy like me in Dannebrog, Nebraska.

Same with good humor. The reason Dorothy is getting growly is that you're having far too much fun. Whatever fun you have has to come from somewhere, and it looks to me like it's coming from Dorothy. The only solution is for you to have a little less fun and for Dorothy to get a good laugh somewhere along the line. I have the feeling that when her lawyer sends out announcements for the auction sale of your tools and tractors, things will definitely even up again.

Dear Mr. Rustoration Answer Man:

My husband has fifteen old Allis-Chalmers WCs cluttering up our yard. I have no idea what he intends to do with all of them. I don't think he knows what he intends to do with them. What's worse, he's making noise about hauling in even more of these rusting, orange derelicts. He has gone beyond all reason. He claims that the tractors are good investments and that he is going to make a lot of money giving other collectors advice about restoration. What do you think?

Distressed Damsel in Dannebrog

Dear Distressed Damsel:

Don't let this guy get away, dearie. What a gem! It sounds to me like he has developed a solid investment program for his family. My impression is that he is working hard for you, asking almost nothing for himself. What a guy! What a sweetheart! I think you should go out to his shop right now and plant a big kiss on his greasy cheek. Boy, are you lucky.

Dear Mr. Rustoration Answer Man Sexist Pig:

Your articles suggest that tractor restoration is a male prerogative. Women drive tractors, collect tractors, restore tractors, repair tractors, and love tractors too. Get your head out of your differential and smell the Liquid Wrench, you chauvinist lug nut.

Feminine in Phillie

Dear Ma'am, Sir:

Your letter was delivered to the wrong address. Please repost your inquiry to Linda, Rural Route, Dannebrog, NE.

Well, that's it for this edition of Mr. Rustoration Answer Man. If you have any questions about tractors, mechanicking, women, or the laws of nature, just drop me a line to my opulent office on the 79th floor of The Rustoration Answer Man Building, Dannebrog NE 68831-9759. You know by now you can count on me.

Before . . .

. . . After.

Chapter 7

Roger's Rules for Full Reality Restoration

Today, we have sources for reproduction parts, books and periodicals, tech guides, and exquisitely detailed restorations—all new concepts. And now, at the cutting edge of restoration, is the latest philosophy—Roger's Rules For Full Reality Restoration.

Up to now, the idea has been to take your tractor back to what it looked like at its perfect moment: The instant it rolled off the assembly line and just before the bozo loading it on the railcar put a ding in the radiator with his lunchbox.

Well, that approach is strictly old hat now. *Full Reality Restoration demands you put your machine in precisely the condition it was in when it was in use on the farm.*

The key to Full Reality Restoration is detail. For example, no one would be dumb enough to try to pass off a tractor as authentic without 8 pounds of baling wire embellishing it. But a few weeks ago I was judging a Full Reality Restoration competition and saw a competitor try to pass off a Case 25/45 as authentic *with a cotter key holding the throttle linkage to the carburetor!*

Details Key to Authenticity

Now, come on! What kind of idiots does this guy take us for? A bit of wire, a bent nail, a galosh buckle, a hairpin maybe, but a cotter key?! Puh-leez!

And the situation got worse. I unscrewed the gas cap and issued demerits because it wasn't a cob wrapped in a sock (extra points for using a brown monkey sock!), which is of course the legitimate way of stopping up a tractor gas tank. Pointing my flashlight down the hole I found . . . Aha! No sticks! No peanut shells! No bitters bottles!! Who's this guy trying to fool?

I should have disqualified the tractor on the spot, but I opened the tractor's toolbox to check for the requisite mouse nest, a frequently forgotten detail. And I found . . . Good grief! There was not only no mouse nest, there were no rusty nuts or broken monkey wrenches! Now, I can understand missing a small detail—like making sure the backside of your monkey wrench is banged up from using it to adjust a magneto or to drive fence staples. But in this case there was no monkey wrench in that toolbox at all. Go figure!

My mind reeled with the disgrace of these Full Reality Restoration oversights, but the horrors continued. The Case had no necking knob on the steering wheel! No Prince Albert can over the exhaust pipe! No gas dripping from the carburetor!

In my days of visiting shows and judging entries, I have seen tractors with the most glaring inconsistencies you can imagine. I once saw a Minnie-Mo UTU with a gearshift knob! Not two weeks ago I saw a McCormick-Deering 10/20 without a wasp nest in the air cleaner! I've seen a Silver King R-66 with an over-the-counter linch pin in the drawbar rather than a bent bolt with the threads bunged up. Oh, the madness! Oh, the humanity!

As an Allis WC man, I was appalled at one "restoration" I saw where the gas tank hadn't been soldered. What kind of "authenticity" is that?! Have you ever seen an Allis-Chalmers WC with a gas tank that hasn't been soldered?

Striving for Respect

If you're going to strive for respect in the circles of Full Reality Restoration, don't skimp on the attention to details like this. Knock the ears off your brass coolant drain plug—not just the easily seen one in the block, but that one tucked up under the radiator. Round off the oil pan drain plug corners. Take off the old filter and screw on a fruit jar stuffed with old jockey shorts. Study old tractors still working out in the fields so you understand the most elusive minutia like this.

Judges aren't going to look at your tractor from a range of twenty yards, you know. Not this judge, at any rate. I'll have on my white gloves and be running a finger along the ground under your tractor to make sure there's at least a minimal, symbolic oil spot there. And that oil better be dirty if you're looking for an award ribbon from ol' Rog!

As an advocate of Full Reality Restoration, I'll be looking at that block with a magnifying glass to make sure it's really cracked—that you haven't tried to sneak one by, scratching a line in the paint with a nail.

Well, I have some work to do on my own tractors—battery acid to spill on a fender, barbed wire to drag along a hood, an iron pipe to weld on a manifold, drain plugs that need to be replaced with bolts, wheel lugs I haven't had a chance to cross-thread.

Sure, it takes work and time. But when I'm done, this baby is going to be as accurate as it can be—a machine just like Grandpa's, straight out of the past!

Chapter 8

Welding With Ol' Rog

Antique tractor restoration is more than a simple matter of getting engines running and repairing a little sheet metal. More even than rebuilding transmissions and adjusting carburetors.

Or timing magnetos, installing new seals and bearings, relining gas tanks, replacing oil pumps, replacing hoses and belts, sealing coolant leaks, cleaning up oil spills, and finding tires. Or replacing rings, inserting shims, drilling out broken studs, cleaning manifolds, checking clogged zirks, scraping carbon, rebuilding distributors, adjusting governors, tweaking chokes, torquing down bolts, gapping rocker arms, seating valves, draining differentials, filling final drives, packing bearings, setting sectors, filing points, cleaning ports, that sort of thing.

No, restoration is more complicated than that. Much more complicated than that. And that's what I love about the hobby. You can't be involved with old iron very long before you find yourself learning things you would never have suspected in your wildest dreams you'd pick up from pounding on stuck pistons or prying at rusted bolts. Before you know it, almost without trying, you'll be picking up all kinds of new things. History, agriculture, geography, economics, dancing, first aid, the intricacies of filing for bankruptcy, and where to find a good marriage counselor, for example.

Take me. This past winter I was working on one of my several Allis-Chalmers WCs, this one the first "styled" model I've worked on. I was to the point of replacing the radiator and cowling when I found a number of tears in the sheet metal and a couple of places where parts of the radiator core had separated from the radiator frame. So, I decided to take a pause in putting the tractor back together until I could learn a little something about soldering.

In the meantime, I decided to turn to my bench to work on the shifter pedestal, transmission forks, and lugs. I found that the little knob on the bottom end of the gear shift lever was so badly worn that it constantly slipped between the lugs, making shifting next to impossible. It was clear it needed to be built up, so I put everything aside, figuring I could return to it when I learned a little something about brazing.

I was about to put the fenders back on but I noticed a couple of the braces were broken and the edges torn. I was about to toss them into the pickup to take them to the local welding shop when it occurred to me, "Rog, it's time to learn how to solder, braze, and weld—right now," and that became my winter's assignment.

And now that I have learned just about everything there is to know about dealing with molten metal, I'm ready to pass the secrets along to you. It's really not all that tough. Look around you at the guys who know how to weld. Not much fodder for the Mensa Society there, right? After all, what kind of person with any sense at all fools around with melted metal, stinky hot leather outfits, and flames and sparks so hot they can melt polar ice caps? Nutty guys, right? Guys like you and me!

Setting Up Shop

The first thing to do is to equip yourself for the task. You'll need a solder gun and solder, a set of oxyacetylene fittings, tanks and valves, an electric welder, a few pounds of brazing rod, welding rod, heavy leather gloves and apron, a welding helmet, an industrial-grade first-aid kit with a special orientation toward third-degree burns, and the biggest fire extinguisher you can find, maybe two.

The most crucial part of a welding shop setup is a good grinder. If you don't show particular talent as a welder, it is particularly important that you become a really good grinder. I'm a great grinder.

You should be able to assemble this basic outfit while spending not much more than the cost of your basic B-1 bomber, without add-ons like a rear spoiler and power windows.

Later you may find that you will also want to:

1) get a variety of skin grafts for the time you used your carbon arc torch while wearing a short sleeve shirt;

2) find someone to put a new roof on the shop after that time it took you *way* too long to get your torch lit;

3) pick up tight-laced boots to replace the open-top shoes you were wearing the time the dime-size glob of molten steel dropped from the pipe you were cutting and precisely into your sock, which is, by the way, where "dancing" comes from in the aforementioned list of the side benefits of tractor restoration; and

4) shop for a seeing-eye dog to compensate for the occasion when it was too hot to wear your helmet so you opted for over-the-counter, nonprescription sunglasses instead.

There are plenty of good books on welding but learning how to weld from a book is like trying to learn about sex from a book. Well, maybe not *exactly* like learning about sex from a book, but you know what I mean.

Constructive Criticism

What's important is to find someone who can weld and doesn't mind you looking over his shoulder. In my case, whenever I finish a practice session with my arc welder, I take my most interesting successes and failures up to the town tavern. Buddies who know how to weld look over my work and offer constructive criticisms and useful advice—like "*Hahahahaha!*" and "*Hoohoohoohoo!*" and "Look at this! He didn't penetrate the first half of the weld and burned through the rest!" and "What a doofus!"

While generous encouragement spurs us on to excellence, in the absence of positive reinforcement, peer humiliation works too. Once when I couldn't hang around, I left a particularly nice weld at the tavern for my welding buddies to critique; the next day Slick the Bartender handed it to me so I could read the inscription someone had written on it in blue pool-cue chalk: "Caution! Fragile! Handle carefully!"

Basically, electric or "arc" welding is a matter of using electricity to melt a steel rod at the same time the furiously hot spark is melting the edges of the metal you are trying to join together. Oxyacetylene does the same thing with burning gases. Various settings on the arc welder—45 amps, 65 amps, 90 amps—make the arc hotter, while adjusting the flame does the same with gas.

The notion is, something mysterious in the gas valves or the arc welding machine agitates electrons something terrible. As I understand it, it calls them "weenies" or shouts at very high speed and volume "Neener neener neener on electrons!" If you put your ear against an arc welder or inhale enough acetylene, you can actually hear the little insults yourself. MiG and TiG welders make the craft of welding far too simple and easy and are therefore reserved for sissies.

Various kinds of welding rod can be used for different results: the number 6012 on the rod, for example, means that, uh, there are exactly 60 somethings in each rod, and one or two of something else, or maybe 12, and it's really good for some jobs, while 6011, or maybe it's 7013, is good for something altogether different . . . but I can't remember exactly.

If you run the amperage or gas too high, everything will melt, including the insulation in your shop attic once the fire spreads. On the other hand, if your spark or flame is too low, your rod sticks, although that sometimes happens if your flux is wet, and frankly, I don't want to talk about that.

Brazing, Soldering, and Other Fine Points

Brazing is done at a lower temperature than welding. Welding happens at something like twelve point six trillion degrees, while brazing is more like twelve point four trillion, and while that may seem like a lot of difference right now, wait until you grab that rod by the wrong end when you're not wearing gloves. Doesn't make a bit of difference. You will use the same language in both cases.

The word "brazing" comes from an old Indo-European word meaning "little yellow beads of melted metal that won't go where you want them to." In brazing, you don't melt the two pieces you are trying to join. The molten metal from the rod is supposed to run between the two pieces like glue (of course, in reality, it runs right on through and permanently joins the pliers you left on the floor to the valve cover you set them on, thinking all the while they'd be safe there).

Soldering is like brazing, except the metal is even softer, melts quicker, and goes into smaller places, like into the little holes your boot laces pass through. Probably most important for you and your insurance agent at this point is that soldering requires fewer skin grafts and smaller fire extinguishers.

There are tons of other things I would like to share with you—like how you shouldn't sit on a gas tank while you're welding it, and how every so often you should lift your helmet and stomp out all the little fires you've accidentally lit around your work area, and how it's not at all a good idea to try to avoid burning holes in your clothes by welding in the nude.

But time is short, and in the meanwhile, I hope my own welding successes encourage you to move on to the wonderful world of metal repair yourself. Don't bother to pat me on the back or shake my hand in gratitude, especially while I'm still in traction and my burns are healing.

Oh, and be careful not to sit on my seeing-eye dog.

Chapter 9

Roger's Rules for Stompin' Around the Junkyard

Probably the second most uncomfortable moment in the tractor restorer's schedule of activities is the inevitable process of negotiating with the local salvage dealer for tractor parts. (The *most* uncomfortable moment is the inevitable process of negotiating with the local salvage dealer's dog over your own body parts.) I can't tell you how often I've been through this ordeal, so I feel I am equipped to offer the veteran as well as the novice some friendly advice.

First, when I take a trip to Jim Stromp's tractor salvage yard, "Stromp's Domp" . . . er, "Dump," near Spalding, Nebraska, not far from my farm, I always carry a pistol. No, not for the dog or for Jim. About a quarter-mile south of Jim's place, I stop my pickup, get out the pistol, and shoot out one of my front tires. That way I can limp into his place, tire flopping, as if I were stopping just to fix my flat.

Rule #1: The last thing in the world you want to do is let a salvage yard proprietor know that you are at his establishment to buy salvage.

While you're fixing your tire, Jim is certain to wander over to see how you're doing, ask about the family, offer you a hand with your bad jack, and, maybe, ask how you're doing with that old tractor you've been restoring for six years. It is really important at this point to show complete confidence, even indifference.

Rule #2: Never let a salvage man like Jim know you're absolutely desperate for a set of power-adjust wheels for a WD Allis-Chalmers.

The thing to do is to say something like, "Oh, hi, Jim. Uh, yeah, the tractor . . . Let's see, that would be the Allis WD. Frankly, I haven't had much time to think about it, Jim. It's just something I fool around in the shop."

At this point, turn away from Jim and concentrate as hard as you can on your jack and that flat tire. "Actually, I'd haul it out of the shop and throw it down in that wash by the creek but the wheels are so rotten I don't think I can even roll it out. I don't suppose you have a couple junk wheels around here that would fit on that machine . . . something to make it easier to drag across the field, would you? Doesn't matter, of course, but what the heck, while I'm here . . . "

Then Jim will say something like, "Hmmm. Power-adjust wheels for an Allis WD, huh? Boy, those things are *really* hard to find. But I think I might just have a couple—in almost mint condition actually— back here behind a shed somewhere."

Now, if you said you needed a ½-inch bolt 3 inches long, standard threads, Jim would say the same thing: "Hmmm. ½-inch bolt 3 inches long, standard threads. Boy, those things are *really* hard to find. But I think I might have one back here somewhere behind the shed somewhere . . . "

Rule #3: Never plan to find parts in a salvage yard in a hurry.

At this point it's absolutely crucial that you slow things down. Play with the jack handle, eat a sandwich, ask Jim about his family, that sort of thing. Then get in a hurry: "Wow, it's three o'clock already. I guess I don't have time to fool around with rusty old wheels today, Jim. Maybe some other time."

Jim's shrewd. He's been here before, probably earlier this very morning, so don't expect him to panic. He may say something like, "Okay, Rog. See ya. Better get some new tires on that truck. And you shouldn't drive around with that loaded pistol."

Okay, get into your truck, put it in gear, say goodbye, and start to roll out of the yard—and then stop. "Hey, Jim, where are those wheels?

I suppose I could take a look at them, while I'm here and all."

As you look at them, make the following things clear without being insulting:

1) you are looking for junk wheels but these things are worse than junk;

2) besides, they don't appear to be the right size for what you need;

3) you don't have any money with you; and

4) you really need to be moving along.

Get back in the truck, start the engine, express your gratitude for Jim's time, mention something about the fact that the manifold you bought from him six weeks ago turned out to be so badly cracked you couldn't use it, and you sure hope no one reports his place to the EPA any time soon.

Start to roll down his driveway. Then, sort of casually, yell over your shoulder, "Hey, Jim, in case I decide to go ahead and use junk wheels, how much do you want for those bent and rusty ones we just looked at?"

As you say the word "those," flick the back of your hand at the two wheels you are by now absolutely lusting for, sitting there behind his shed.

He'll say something ridiculous like "$300 each, and I'm losing money at that price, but since you're an old friend and all . . . "

Don't let him finish the sentence. Pop your clutch and kill the engine as if you're so astonished by this obscene figure that you've actually lost control of your body. Some fellows pee their pants at this point, but that may be carrying the strategy a bit far, especially if you're sitting in your own truck.

Rule #4: Don't become insulting at this point.

Let Jim know that you are surprised, but of course he knows his business and has always been scrupulously fair in such matters, but that you're just surprised that these pieces of rusted crap have roughly the same value as gold ingots. Make it clear that $300 *for the pair* is so far beyond your means that these wheels of his are out of the question.

Rule #5: When it comes down to final negotiations, blame everything on a friend because somewhere a friend is at this very moment blaming something on you. Tell Jim that you have a friend who is also looking for two power-adjust wheels for his WD and he's an idiot and he might be willing to pay something along the lines of $100.

"$100 a piece, surely," Jim will say.

"Both," you will reply.

At this point the negotiation becomes automatic. You offer less, he demands more, on and on, and eventually you'll come close to closing. And here is where the process gets too complicated to cover in detail.

Did you, for example, filch a carburetor or magneto and stash it under the seat of your truck when Jim wasn't looking? Did Jim spot you filching parts during your last visit so he is tacking on the price of the air cleaner and distributor cap on these wheels (or for that matter the water pump and belt pulley you tossed behind your toolbox while he was answering the phone ten minutes ago)? Or, does he feel a slight twinge of guilt about sticking you with the bent crankshaft you paid a prime price for last December, or does he know one of the two wheels you're looking at right now is so twisted you'll never get it onto the tractor hub?

Whatever the case, you'll eventually arrive at something like $140 for the pair—Jim will throw in sixteen lug nuts (six of which will turn out to have left-hand threads and therefore be of no use whatsoever to you).

Then Jim figures your tab, adding sales tax, value-added tax, cartage, ullage, and import fees, amounting to, let's see here, exactly $182. You'll fumble around in your pocket like a brother-in-law when it's time to buy a round and announce that all you have with you is precisely $152.73, two largish cotter pins, and a slightly bent lock washer but that maybe you could come back in a month or two and look at the wheels again. Jim will quickly take your cash, pins, and washer.

Rule #6: Every parts transaction is the groundwork for the next transaction.

Load up the wheels, doing your best to look just a little grumpy, so you'll have some basis for your negotiations in a few weeks when you're back looking for a right fender. You can be sure Jim will have something to say about how it's pretty tough making a living selling things at a loss every day and how he doesn't know how he'd send the kids to college if it weren't for his economy in saving cotter pins and washers after deals like this.

Rule #7: When the dust settles, every deal is a good deal.

As you leave the yard, Jim will compliment you on what a tough bargainer you are, thinking all the while that at supper he'll tell the family how he nailed you $152.73 for a couple wheels he thought he'd eventually haul to the scrap yard, and of course you'll whistle all the way home, planning to impress your spouse with the story of how you picked up two wheels in mint condition for less than Myron Freeble paid last week for a rusted-out one he wound up using for a mailbox stand.

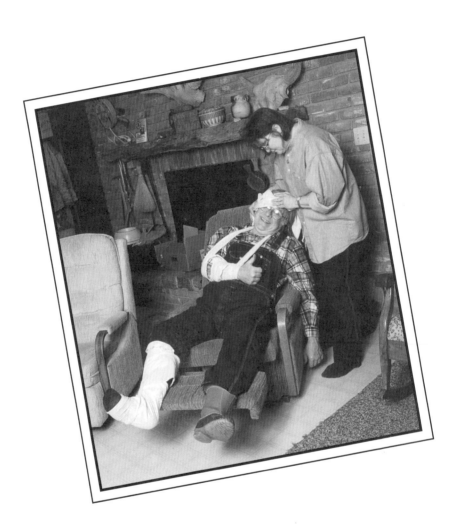

Chapter 10

In Sickness and in Health, Until Debt Do You Part . . .

As most of my friends will tell you, especially those who are mechanics, I'm not much of a mechanic. The problem is, when I met and married my Lovely Linda seventeen years ago, I wasn't any kind of mechanic at all, except maybe a word mechanic.

It has been, in fact, only seven or eight years since I first applied a crescent wrench to a stuck oil pan plug and caught the antique tractor restoration bug that has infected me so badly ever since. And believe me, dismantling and reassembling an old, broken-down paragraph is nothing like tearing down and overhauling a stuck tractor engine, no matter what your English teachers told you.

I have never been a fussy, cautious sort of fellow but I can tell you for a fact, neither was I ever in the first half-century of my life as consistently, thoroughly, and enthusiastically filthy, bloody, battered, and, well, as *content* as I have been since I started developing a shop full of tools, a yard full of rusty iron, a life full of tractor friends. . . .

And a wife full of fear, compassion, and home remedies.

Tractor-Restorer Restorer

That's how Linda is my partner in tractor restoration: She is, when I think about it, a tractor-restorer restorer—repairing me after I've been repairing tractors. The most obvious and frequent task Linda faces when I return to the house from a day in the shop stems from my natural and total lack of grace.

When I was in high school, the basketball coach summed things up pretty well when he said after one practice, "Welsch, what you lack in coordination, you make up in clumsiness." I would have argued with him, but something got caught between my feet—in fact, it *was* one of my feet, now that I think of it—and I fell down.

My youthful talents have apparently extended into my old age. Most of them, anyway. As a result, it is the rare evening when I come staggering back to the house and to Linda without a variety of self-inflicted burns, contusions, abrasions, and lacerations.

And that's when I've been writing something in my office.

When I return from the shop, it is as often as not in the company of a couple members of the Dannebrog EMTs and a couple researchers investigating freak accidents for the *New England Journal of Medicine.*

Encountering Carbon Monoxide

I think, for example, of the not-so-funny time I was working on a tractor in the shop and needed to start it up. Now, I'm a man of some experience and common sense. I was, after all, a professor for thirty-five years. No dummy, me. So, I figure you can't run a tractor in a closed shop for much more than a quarter-hour or so before carbon monoxide will start doing its ugly work.

Duh . . . carbon monoxide kills in minutes. Luckily, however, I'm a German and, after thousands of years of my people eating sauerkraut and weisswurst, my system is pretty much immune to gases that are deadly to less-resistant peoples. So, after five or six minutes, instead of just lying down and dying like any decent Swede or Brazilian would have done, I caught myself headed toward the floor, figured out this wasn't a case of just taking another stumble, and somehow got out the door into the clean, fresh Nebraska air. I managed to get the tractor turned off and the shop aired out and then I went to the house to sit down and check in with Nurse Linda.

Of course, like any nervous woman, Linda wanted to call the doctor and get competent, educated medical advice. And I, like any reasonable man, said absolutely not; we could just wait and see if I fell down again. She, like any nervous woman who is married to a reasonable man, went ahead and called the doctor anyway. Their conversation, as I recall, went like this:

Linda: "Is he going to die?"

Doc Lawton: "If he's up and around, he's probably all right, but keep an eye on him. Give me another call if he gets to acting goofy later tonight."

Linda: "Regular goofy or special goofy? He acts goofy every night."

Doc Lawton: "Well, then let me know if he starts acting unusual . . . like, as if he has any common sense at all."

Linda: "Will do. I shouldn't have any trouble spotting bizarre behavior like that."

Take Up a Lighter Hobby

It was almost certainly events like this—or the time I put my hand directly into the flame of a cutting torch, or maybe the time I dropped a transmission on my foot, or perhaps the time I got my hair permanently snarled in the wheels of my creeper—that brought Linda to the point of exclaiming in the presence of my friend and CBS producer Bud Lamoreaux as they watched me working on a main bearing under a tractor up on jacks, "I just wish Roger had a hobby that didn't weigh so much!"

Whereupon Bud put the whole issue to rest by asking, "You mean like maybe a hobby weighing 120 pounds, with high heels and long, blond hair?"

So much for that discussion! Linda never again brought up how unsafe it is to work under a ton and a half of cold iron.

Over the last few years, therefore, Linda has acquired a fairly extensive inventory of first-aid supplies. In fact, the last time there was a disaster exercise in the nearby large city of Grand Island, the hospital, as part of their preparedness check, called Linda to see if she could maybe help them out by bringing in some of her Band-Aids, splints, iodine, swabs, compresses, disinfectant, sutures, and chocolate-chip cookies. (No matter how badly I'm injured, we've discovered, a couple chocolate-chip cookies always help.)

In fact, when it comes right down to it, the most important treatment in Linda's medical cabinet is her boundless ability to say "There, there," pat me on the shoulder, and tell me that maybe things will be better tomorrow. Like maybe the burns won't still be smoking and skin will heal over the bone. No matter how dumb I've been—dropping a floor jack on my head, cutting myself with a hammer, burning myself with a gear puller—Linda always manages to come up with something soothing to say: "There, there—did that nasty jack jump up and bonk you on the head, you poor dear?! Here, have a chocolate-chip cookie."

In fact, when it comes right down to it, maybe one of the best things about working in the shop is that I can always be sure that no matter how bad I smell when I come back to the house, no matter how exhausted I am from what is essentially a waste of time, no matter how much this latest project is going to cost, no matter how frustrated I am, or injured, Lovely Linda is always there to cool my fevered brow, soothe my battered spirits, and staunch my spurting veins, to rub my forehead, bind my wounds, and bring me chocolate-chip cookies.

In fact, when it comes right down to it, that old injury to my left foot is starting to act up . . . and boy, does that ever hurt! And that burn on my left hand isn't healing all that well—I'll bet it's getting infected. And maybe I breathed in a little too many solvent fumes today; I'm feeling a little woozy. Maybe I should go back to the house so Linda can check to make sure I'm OK.

In fact, when it comes right down to it, I'm sure I should! "Linda! Linda! I think I hurt myself again! Oh, Linda . . . ! And don't forget the cookies!"

Chapter 11

The Intangibles

Sure, you need tools, a workbench, cabinets, chests, jacks and racks, bins and shelves for the super shop. Yes, you need to plan space for compressors, welding tanks, hoists, and scrap. Of course, you need lighting, safety devices, heat, and stools.

But let's face it, a shop is more than a place to repair things. A *real* shop is a retreat, where you play as much as you work, a place of comfort and pleasure, home for the soul *and* the saw.

Location, Location, Location

As is the case with all real estate, the three most important things about your shop are 1) location, 2) location, and 3) location. Remember Tim Allen's television show *Home Improvement*? Remember how his workshop was just out the door from his wife's kitchen? Remember how stupid you thought that was? The producer of this show was definitely not someone who ever had anything to do with a shop! Man, if there is one place you *don't* want your shop, it's just off the household kitchen. Maybe 200 yards off the household kitchen, but not just outside the door. The inevitable exchange of aromas alone is not good for either work area, believe me.

The outside of your shop should be suitably intimidating so no one will just drop in to see what you're doing. My shop door, for example, has a sign saying:

DANGER
Deadly Manure Gases Possible
Death may be immediate
Enter pit only with:
Self-contained air supply,
Ventilation
Rescue harness, mechanical lift, and stand-by person

A sign like that pretty much does the job of keeping away children, insurance salesmen, posses, and tool borrowers.

On the other hand, the inside of your shop should be comfortable to the point of opulence. If I could, I'd have something by way of a recliner chair, but I've never had much luck with upholstered furniture in my shop. Enough kerosene, crankcase oil, solvent, and Liquid Wrench tends to transfer from my overalls to the upholstery to convert the chair into something roughly as explosive as the Big Boy atomic bomb of World War II. Eventually, a cat won't even sleep on it.

Other than that, when it comes to shop comfort, the sky's the limit. I have a small television set in my shop. Not so big that it lures in the weekend football crowd but big enough so I can see the smile on Little Al's face when he roars across yet another finish line.

On the other hand, you want the biggest sound system you can afford, because if you turn it up loud enough, anyone who isn't scared off by the sickle blades and rusted mufflers piled up around the door just may be frightened away when they see the walls of your shop puff in and out to the bass beat of ZZ Top playing "Sharp Dressed Man" (a song I've always suspected they wrote specifically for me).

Interior decoration for the shop is, of course, a matter of individual taste. I have always been partial to girlie calendars, Indy posters, and pictures of things closest to my heart: Stilton cheese, black Labs, and

Antonia's drawings of her dad at work. Some mechanics hang photos of their family above the workbench, since if they have a really great shop, they are not likely to see much of them otherwise.

Unwelcome Guests

Several of my friends have a refrigerator in their shops. Not a good idea. Add a cot and you are simply begging to hear the words from your spouse, "Well, you have it so blasted cozy out here, why don't you just go ahead and stay here all night?!" It's better not to make that kind of invitation too easy to issue, if you catch my drift.

Also, if you actually have some serious notions about getting something done in your shop, the last thing you want is a fridge full of cold beer, pop, and sandwich materials. You can just about count on six or eight buddies moving in, along with their cots and sleeping bags, or worse yet, just stopping by and leaving not only with an armload of borrowed tools and spare parts, but also a hamper full of picnic makings.

On the other hand, snacks that can be disguised as gasket material or concealed in transmission cases can be a real comfort to the mechanic in his shop. I strongly urge secure containers, however, since I once had a resident mouse empty several bags of unshelled peanuts in my shop, haul them away and stash them in various tractor orifices. These he ate at his leisure, stuffing the shells into radiators, differentials, carburetors, crankcases, distributors, and tool drawers, where I am still finding them years later. At least he was tidy and didn't throw them on the floor.

Lamentably, my shop is placed in such a way that I can't have one of our dogs out there as a resident or even as a temporary visitor. That's too bad. Nothing makes a shop more cozy than a good dog. Preferably a big dog. Ideally, a big, black dog.

For a shop companion, I have had to settle for a tailless cat named Cindy Clawford. She came tailless; it was not, as many of my friends maintain, another example of my mechanicking.

Cindy hasn't worked out quite the way I'd hoped: she does catch mice and snakes, but unfortunately, she doesn't catch them in the shop and take them outside. She catches them outside in the yard and brings them into the shop.

Moreover, she seems comfortable enough with my tools, parts, and tractors, but she is terrified by me, especially when something blows up or I drop a large piece of sheet metal. In such cases she tends to exit abruptly by way of the ceiling ventilator, and Linda has to lure her back toward the house in a week or so when she finally ventures home from the other side of the river.

An Aromatic Atmosphere

Cindy's aversion to me may also be what I consider one of the single most important, most neglected elements of the perfect shop: bouquet. Like a good wine, a shop needs just the right "nose." In my shop, there is the underlying piquancy of Liquid Wrench with a distinct overlay of stale transmission grease. Not to be ignored, however, is the suggestion of rotting rubber and a lingering but ephemeral trace of welding fumes. Some visitors insist they detect just a trace of antifreeze and maybe scorched hair, but more distinct is an element of fresh Band-Aids and blasphemy. And a touch of dead snake and wet cat.

Again, a matter of personal taste.

So, sure, fix up your shop, paint the floors, make little outlines on the walls for tools, label the cans and jars, arrange everything neatly and conveniently. But be sure not to ignore the really important things—those intangibles.

Chapter 12

Ageless Iron Olympics

The notion of "athletics" and "sports" has experienced an inflation not unlike me every year between Thanksgiving and Christmas. The Olympics take a lot more time these days because right along with running, jumping, lifting, and throwing, there are sports like competitive tap dancing and interior decorating. Currently scheduled for the next Olympics are a flower-arranging heptathalon, metric embroidery (mixed doubles), and Greco-Roman sneezing.

And I think that's fine. The only problem is that some of us have been left out. Somewhere along the line those of us who love old tractors have fallen out of the loop. I am, therefore, proposing to the International Olympic Committee that they consider adding the following events to the international competition as soon as possible . . . or at least before I'm too old to compete.

Rusty Rear Wheel Lug, 24-Inch Breaker Bar Speed Competition: From a standing start, contestants break loose and remove four of five rear, 1-inch wheel lugs. One lug will be welded in place; one lug will be loose and coated with graphite. Style points will be deducted for hernias and broken noses.

Two-Pound Wrench Throw: This event is planned as a consolation follow-up for the previous event. Contestants who incur hernias or broken noses will be able to regain lost style points by throwing the offending wrench for distance. Additional style points can be obtained if the athlete's ensuing curses continue through the entire flight of the wrench, including its bounces to a final rest somewhere close to the back fence lilac bushes.

Drecko-Slimin' Transmission Wrestling and Cross-Country Run: Contestants will remove a thoroughly greased transmission from a tractor and squat-carry it 15 feet across a shop, around an engine stand and between two floor jacks, stepping over a variety of ball bearings, twelve-point sockets, and broken bolts scattered at random around the floor.

Three-Man Engine Timing: This is, clearly, a team event. National squads will approach a four-cylinder machine. While a bottom man opens the flywheel vent and turns it to top-center fire position, the other two team members will open the magneto and timing gear case. All three will at all times scream contradictory instructions at each other. At least one member of the team during the competition will get a finger caught in the timing gear; at least one second member will clearly show judges that he has finger-tested the magneto by a display of standing hair, flaring nostrils, and glowing eyeballs.

Lock Washer Polo: The contestant has seven minutes to shuffle a ½-inch lock washer around a shop floor, keeping it well out of the reach of three opponents trying to pick the blasted thing up. The goal will be to deposit the washer down a crack behind a shop cabinet where it will remain for the next fifty years, until the building burns down, or until it simply disappears mysteriously forever.

Two-Man Bidding: Two opponents compete by bidding for a salvage tractor at auction, not exceeding the actual value of the wreckage by more than 50 percent, the point at which the overbidder will be disqualified.

Consequential Cringing and Prevarication: The winner of the previous competition will perform a timed pick up and hauling of the purchased metallic rubble, trucking or trailering it 200 yards to the Spousal Cringe and Prevaricate Pit, where he/she will attempt to justify the purchase and save the marriage. Point deductions for not keeping a straight face while explaining the buy.

Individual Crank Starts and Flywheel Spins: Contestants attempt to start, one after the other for a timed result, six tractors, three of which will have flywheel starts, three of which will have crank starts, and one of which will have a defective impulse. Survivors will be cleaned up, carried to a whirlpool tub, and given three weeks free physical therapy or a full body cast, depending.

Cross-Country Woodlot Scanning: Teams of three drive through heavily worked agricultural land in a pickup truck. Without scanners, metal detectors, or binoculars, the teams find, negotiate for, and load as many pre-1950 tractors, implements, or parts as possible. Style points deducted for poison ivy, barbed-wire cuts, and imbedded shotgun pellets.

Precision Torquing: Individual Olympians torque down an entire tractor's worth of nuts and bolts with standard breaker bar and sockets. Judges then check torques with torque wrenches. Highest degree of accuracy wins; lowest degree has to pull piston rods out of engine blocks.

Synchronized Dolly Floor Exercise: Teams of five, eight, and twelve mechanics perform pre-choreographed routines on floor dollies to one (1) country-western tune, one (1) classical piece, and one (1) rock-and-roll song while completely lubing and changing the oil in an antique tractor selected by the Ageless Iron Olympic Committee. Awards decided on the basis of the most torn ligaments, strained muscles, bruises, and stitches.

Ten-Item Checkbook Balance: This is a mixed-gender, team competition between a husband and wife. The spouse most deeply involved in tractor collecting, restoration, parts or tool buying purchases ten items and conceals the purchases in a checkbook record in such a way that his/her spouse cannot find more than five of the expenditures in a ten-minute period.

And frankly, that's just a start. I foresee a time when *most* Olympic events will deal with antique tractors, implements, and tools. In fact, I imagine that sooner or later participants in goofy activities like running, jumping, throwing, tatting, and hair teasing will be asking to join in on *our* fun.

Chapter 13

Ageless Iron Horoscopes

Up until a few years ago, I pretty much dismissed horoscopes as being superstitious nonsense. But then I read one that shook me right down to my size 12s (and in case you are wondering, those are my shoes).

It was my birthday and it was my horoscope for the year. It read, "Women find you attractive, almost irresistible. You are creative and entertaining. You are generous to a fault and have beautiful children. Your future success seems assured because it is. Scorp, you go for it. There's nothing you can't do if you really want to."

Uncanny, isn't it? It's almost as if this woman lived in our house, she knows me so well. How could she do that if there weren't something to astrology? It was enough to convince me.

At any rate, I have plotted some planets, shot an azimuth, calculated cusps and conjunctions—even a couple of expletives—and have come up with the following cosmic truths for you (for entertainment purposes only, of course).

Aquarius (January 20–February 18): You are noted for your generosity, which is why your brother-in-law borrows tools and you never see them again. Your strong point is that you sometimes throw things away, which you certainly wouldn't do if you were a Scorpio, and I can tell you that for a fact.

Pisces (February 19–March 20): You are a dreamer, fish-fellow. You're never going to find the Rumely OilPull you want, so forget it and settle on the Allis WC your wife said you could go ahead and pull out of the neighbor's woodlot. Water is your element, and that's why your radiators all leak.

Aries (March 21–April 19): You are enthusiastic and determined, which is why you got into trouble a couple years ago stalking that widow who wouldn't sell you her late husband's Ford 8N. Your sign is the ram, which pretty much describes the subtlety of your tractor restoration techniques. When you get hold of a live spark plug wire, you don't let go.

Taurus (April 20–May 20): Your sign is a bull, which pretty much explains why no one bids against you at a tractor auction. You are generally barred from entering china shops, and even NAPA stores. Your lucky tractor is a dozer.

Gemini (May 21–June 21): Your lucky tractor, on the other hand, Mr. Double-Dealer, is either the Twin City or a John Deere B, not only because it has twin cylinders but because Geminis tend to be a little slow but can usually figure out the firing order on these machines. You usually have to do things twice to get them right. At least twice.

Cancer (June 22–July 22): You always know the firing order. In fact, you always know *everything*. You, after all, are the crab, and nothing is ever right. No, that isn't *exactly* the right color for an Empire, but it's the best I could do. Yes, I checked the setting on the torque wrench. I don't care if you think it is too warm in my shop. You make enemies easily and don't get a lot of invitations to tractor club meetings.

Leo (July 23–August 22): Your sign is the lion, and you usually are. You know as well as I do that you didn't once buy a high-crop John Deere in mint condition for $35 from a guy who thought it was scrap iron. No, I don't believe that you can figure tolerances to $\frac{1}{1,000}$ of an inch with your fingernails.

Virgo (August 23–September 22): You have a hard time concentrating, which is why you own two John Deeres, an Allis-Chalmers, most of an International, and if I'm not mistaken, that's an Oliver 88 hood on your Case.

Libra (September 23–October 23): You are easygoing and tend to put things off. When a wrench slips and you bust your knuckles, you don't cuss for two hours. Your lucky color is rust, which describes most of your tractors because you never get around to painting them.

Scorpio (October 24–November 21): Scorp, babe, you are irresistible to women. You write like Shakespeare. You tend to be headstrong but, hey, you're usually right! You are honest, brave, thrifty, reverent and true—especially if you were born on November 6.

Sagittarius (November 22–December 21): Your very name comes from the word "sage," which means that you are a thinker—and that you like turkey dressing. You spend a lot of time sitting in the shop thinking, as a matter of fact, with a beer in one hand and a naughty-girl magazine in the other. But hey, that's thinking—sort of.

Capricorn (December 22–January 19): Your sign is an old goat, and you don't need me to help you figure that one out. When not bothering women-folk, you are banging your head against a wall. You're the kind of guy who actually thinks he can fix a magneto. At tractor auctions, the auctioneer loves you. You'll bid $4,444.36 on a John Deere B with no magneto, carburetor, radiator, pistons, or wheels.

Rog:
Steer to
the right.

Antonia:
To the
right?

Rog:
No, the
other right!

Chapter 14

_____

Tractor Hauling Hand Signals

I've now been working on old tractors darn near ten years. And daughter Antonia is now seventeen. That means, well, do the math, she's been helping me move machinery since she was a mere seven years old.

Originally, I put her on the haulee tractor rather than the hauler, and about all she had to do was handle the steering wheel. But she got tired of the explosions, smoke, heat, roaring, and flying parts—and that was only from *me*—so now she drives the puller and I wrestle whatever wreckage we are hauling. So I am the one who winds up with the blackened hands, sore muscles, and rusty butt.

As always, I approached this activity as a scholar, scientist, and practical mechanic (which is to say, I'm practically a mechanic). Because of the inevitable din of our puller tractor, the tearing of metal, wrenching of gears, and rattle of falling parts on the pullee, I have devised a set of hand signals with which I can indicate to Antonia what I have in mind and she can respond with signs telling me her questions, confusion, or contempt.

I hope these help you as much as they have helped us. For one thing, it has encouraged Antonia to excel in school. So she can get scholarships. So she can go a long ways away to school. A long, long, *long* ways away.

Antonia:
Your instructions
are not clear.

Rog:
I'm
doing
my best.

Antonia:
Is the tractor
supposed
to be tipping
like this?

Rog:
No,
that's because
you just ran
over a sickle bar
and ruined
a tire.

Antonia:
I don't care
if I ever sit on
tractor wreckage
again the rest
of my life.

Rog:
But I really
need your
help on this!
Would $5
help?

Antonia:
Make it $10
and we're
back in
business.

Antonia:
I'm ready
when you are.

Rog:
Women!

Dave Mowitz and Rog toast the
Allis-Chalmers fender love seat.

Chapter 15

Inferior Decorating

You've seen them across the American countryside. Old tractors, rusting and battered. But I'm not talking here about tractors abandoned in woodlots to rust away. No, I'm thinking about machinery arrayed purposely in front yards as decorative elements. Of course there are new tractors out front too these days, again not simply parked and waiting to be put into service as an agricultural tool, but as objects of respect and admiration. Let's face it: A lot of us regard old tractors as things of beauty.

So, how about taking this wonderful idea one more, logical step forward and introducing tractors and tractor parts as *interior* decorative elements into our homes and office? Now, the illustrations here are only suggestions and I have not a doubt in my mind that with the creative spirits that inspire every aspect of old tractor collection, you are going to do even better. Just give me credit when you show off your handiwork. You know, something like: Yes, I did create this John Deere steering pedestal floor lamp in my own shop, but (here's the important part) *I got the idea from that wonderful writer, Roger Welsch.*

Tractor-seat garden-ornament bird.

Barn-pulley swans.

Garden ornaments.

Planter.

Hay-hook planter.

Chapter 16

Shop Security

Security is a concern every shop owner must consider in these days of decreasing respect for other people's property—disappearing tools, equipment, vehicles. Let's face it: Nothing is safe as long as you live in the same town as your brother-in-law.

Your first line of defense against thievery and vandalism is your common, everyday telephone. Don't answer it. When your buddy calls from up the road and asks, "Say, old pal, do you still have that floor jack and jackstand set you got last Christmas?" you know as well as I do that you're about to lose your floor jack and jackstands.

If one of the kids or your wife answers the phone and won't lie for you (why is it they'll lie about the dent in the fender or the cost of a dress but feel the irresistible urge to be honest when someone wants to borrow a tool?), then you have to take another direction. I recommend that you respond, "Uh, no, I don't. You borrowed it shortly after New Year's Eve."

Even if he didn't borrow it shortly after New Year's Eve, he is going to be slow to admit he doesn't have it because for all he knows, considering how he's dealt with other stuff he's borrowed from you, he's probably broken or lost it, or loaned it to someone else.

(Shop Tip: Some experts in this area recommend that you take a proactive position by asking immediately, "By the way, do you still have that valve spring compressor you borrowed from Bob last year?" Now it's your friend's turn to lie!)

You will find that if you do this very often, your borrowin' buddies will catch on. They won't call anymore—they'll just stop by when the shop door is open or the lights are on. Now they can see the jack and stands, so your options are considerably limited. A good strategy in this event is to say, "Sure, you can borrow them. *I don't like to use this cheesy Hong Kong jack anymore now that Eric has that really great, heavy-duty, Snap-On set-up.*" Your borrowing friend will move on. No one likes to work with cheap tools.

Effective Signage

Your next line of defense is signage. Along with your "Keep Out," "No Trespassing," and "No Gurls" signs, you will want to put up radiation, mad dog, and land mine warnings. Even this may not discourage the most determined borrower, however, especially once they learn that all they have to do to divert the dogs is ask, "Where's your Frisbee?"

I have had good luck for short periods of time, especially with strangers, with a couple great signs I got from Gempler's Farm Supply. One warns splendidly, "Danger! Deadly Manure Gases Possible! Death May Be Immediate!" This has the advantage of being largely true. You can get a bulk discount by buying several of these items, to be given as Christmas presents. The one I gave Eric to put on the men's room door up at the tavern has, he figures, saved him from six or seven lawsuits.

The Gempler's sign that has been most successful for me, however, has been the one that reads, "Danger! These Monkeys Bite and Cause Serious Injuries! Do Not Approach!" It's interesting to me as an anthropologist that people who go right by signs that say, "Keep Out!" "No Visitors Please," "Stop," or "Guard Dogs on Duty," walk slowly backward, eyeing the trees in our yard, when faced with the potential of being attacked by crazed monkeys.

Smoke Screens

A natural for a security zone arises in most shops when it comes to wives trying to find someone to fix the washer, clean the attic, or have a fun afternoon in town taking in that wonderful romantic comedy movie everyone has been talking about.

Most farm shops by their very nature produce sufficient smell, noise, smoke, and dirt to repel dogs and hogs, not to mention wives and daughters. Just in case, however, I suggest that you keep ready at all times a large hammer and piece of sheet metal to bang on, a small tin of oil-soaked rags that can be ignited to set up an immediate and temporary smudge, and a standard hand lotion dispenser full of used motor oil that can be quickly smeared onto forearms and face as a repellent.

(Shop Tip: A filthy shop apron presoaked in black oil, solvent, and mud is another helpful and quick visitor disguster. Keep one handy!)

I do not share the conventional enthusiasm for livestock as security devices. Most dogs I've known would welcome a midnight visit from a thief, signal clearly to borrowing buddies that you are in the shop and receiving guests, but bark loud and long at someone like the UPS man delivering your latest tool order, thus calling the attention of those in the house, if you catch my drift, to your most recent extravagance.

Should Heather Locklear show up to ask your advice for installing O-rings on a new cylinder sleeve on an Allis-Chalmers WC, you can bet your dog will bite her. I have no direct evidence of this, but there isn't a doubt in my mind. I know my dogs. I know my luck when it comes to Heather Locklear.

Under *no* circumstances should you install a shop cat. I thought this would be a good idea too, and so I cut a hole in the shop door a few years ago for my ex-shop cat Cindy Clawford. I was pleased that almost every day she presented me with a dead mouse until I discovered that she wasn't really catching the mice in the shop. She was catching them outside and bringing the carcasses into the shop so I could step on them when I came in the door before I turned on the lights.

Cindy is now our *garage* cat; she likes to walk up the back of our cars with muddy feet and then slide down the windshields on a kind of kitty ski slope. Gosh, I sure hope I don't run over her sometime when I'm backing up real fast and her food dish is coincidentally under the back wheels!

Detectors and Alarms

I have carbon monoxide and smoke detectors in my shop, both of which seem to go off primarily when I've eaten an anchovy-and-pepperoni pizza for lunch. I also have a yard light right outside the front door of the shop, which should help thieves avoid injury while they are loading their truck with my equipment and tools.

(Shop Tip: I have padlocks on all the doors of my shop; I find that locks I have cut off with bolt cutters because I've lost the keys make excellent fishing sinkers!)

A couple years ago I bought and installed inexpensive light-and-motion detectors in my shop. When they sense anybody moving about in your shop (simply opening the door will set them off) or turning on the lights, or even using a flashlight, they instantly turn on glaring, blinding floodlights and emit a piercing siren. Any unsuspecting intruder is almost certain to be startled into panicked flight, probably running into doors and equipment, possibly inflicting considerable physical injury on himself, and dropping any tools or weapons in his hands.

The resultant disturbance will awaken the dogs and set them to barking and wake up anyone sleeping in the house so the intruder can be confronted and punished.

That's what happens to me every time I go in there, anyway.

Chapter 17

Adventures in Toolboxes

It's easy enough to figure out the limitations of the tool inventory best suited for the conventional work, farm, professional, or hobby shop: You buy all the tools and equipment you can within your ability to pay for them, accommodate them to the room you have, and sneak them past the wife without her spotting them on the charge card or check stubs. The real problem comes when you are faced with an emergency and you're not *in* the shop, or even near it.

Household problems are a special category for me because I have argued for ten years now that tractor tools are highly specialized and will not work on such things as a mouse in the furnace, an entire spool of Christmas ribbon wound around the brushes of a vacuum sweeper, or the two cotter keys and a 4/10 shotgun shell stuck under a washing machine agitator.

My position has always been that you have to use the right tool for the right job. A large screwdriver to cut the head off of a stubborn rivet or a chisel to tighten the screws in a door hinge, for example, and tractor tools are *not* household tools.

Early on in our marriage, therefore, I gave Linda a nice little toolbox with a variety of standard tools in it as a special present. She was really happy with the sentiment, of course, and since Valentine's Day fell on a week day that year, it wasn't all that much trouble to run into town and buy her some chocolates and flowers yet that morning.

At any rate, this arrangement has really been handy for us. Instead of her saying, "Rog, why don't you grab a hammer and screwdriver and do something about the screen door that fell off the back porch," which would then require me to spend an hour looking and then report that I can't find a hammer and screwdriver, but that I'll fix it sometime next week when I find same, I can tell her, "Linda, just get out your toolbox and fix it yourself."

Then she says to me, "I can't find my hammer and screwdriver because you borrowed them three weeks ago to pry open a can of sardines and I haven't seen them since." And then I can spend an hour looking for them and then report that I can't find them but that I'll fix it sometime next week when I find same.

Individual Needs

My buddy Dan carries about forty pounds of extra tools in his pockets. But then he's a plumber and needs the ballast. Watching him sort out enough change to buy a beer at the tavern is a major production, and worth watching—tools, parts, foreign coins, plumbing parts, sinks, fishing rods—you never know what he's going to pull out of there.

When I travel, I always have a Swiss army knife and a Leatherman tool thingie in my suitcase, and those things have paid for themselves many times over. But they are never available for the single most common need I have, which is to say, when I forget or lose the keys to my suitcase. In which case the tools are inside the suitcase. The *locked* suitcase.

Even worse in regard to on-the-spot tools is the occasion when something goes wrong with a vehicle when you are nowhere near your shop. I carry a full complement of tools in my vehicles and on my tractors for just such an emergency. It would be foolish to do otherwise. For example, my pickup truck Blue Thunder's butterfly valve in the carburetor sticks. It usually does this at the post office, whenever there's a crowd gathered out front. That way everyone can stand around and make comments when I use a jack handle to pry open the hood, barbecue tongs to unscrew the thumbscrew off the top of the air breather, and then jam the broken broomstick I always carry in the cab into the throat of the blasted thing.

Which works.

Then I leap from the truck before the engine dies, pull the broomstick from the carburetor, throw the cover back on the air cleaner, slam down the hood, refasten it with baling wire and a bungee cord or two, and drive off, often to the general applause of the gathered admirers.

The Complete Inventory

Probably the most impressive portable tool inventory carried anywhere other than a Snap-On truck is in any woman's purse. During my long life I have seen women free up jammed elevator assemblies in skyscrapers, jack a derailed locomotive back onto the tracks, rewire a faulty hard drive in a laptop computer, and repair broken rotors in an airliner jet engine—while in flight!—using only tools they just happened to find in the bottom of their purses.

I now urge men to amuse and amaze themselves by playing a little game I have come up with during idle hours. When you find yourself whiling away hours stranded in some airport or doctor's waiting room or retirement investment seminar, lean over to a woman, any woman, within reach and ask her something like, "You wouldn't happen to have something in your purse I could use as a valve spring compressor, do you?'

It doesn't matter what you ask for, of course. Vary your requests; it makes the game all the more fun. "By any chance do you have something I could use to free a stuck shell casing from this mortar tube?" "Would you by any chance have a calf puller I could borrow for a few minutes?" "I seem to have misplaced my cement trowel . . . do you have one handy?" "Excuse me . . . stupid me . . . I came to the airport without an engine hoist . . . would you happen to . . . ?"

Now, notice carefully what follows: The lady will not *look* in her purse. First she will heft it. Yes, she has the engine hoist but she doesn't have the valve spring compressor. But that's okay, she usually uses an eyelash pruner for that job anyway and she knows for a fact it'll work just fine.

Of course she has a mortar tube cleaning tool. In fact, exactly what caliber is your mortar? And there's an engine hoist in there somewhere. She can tell all that from the *weight* of her tote. Then she'll shake it. From the *sound* she'll be able to tell that she has the 2-inch coarse-thread bolts you asked for, but not the metric. (But don't you worry: She can rethread what she has with her nail clippers.)

"Here," she will say to you, handing you a jackhammer. "Let me check for the trowel. I'm sure there's one in here somewhere . . . "

She will then *feel* in her handbag for the weed whacker you asked about, and still not looking, produce two. And a spool of replacement cutting line, just in case.

Chapter 18

The Nebraska Testing Facility: True Advocates for Tractor Buyers

The story has become legend: Unsuspecting farmers, unfamiliar with this remarkable new technology of internal combustion engines and tractors but wanting to be a part of the agricultural revolution, trusted in a name—and bought themselves Ford tractors, invented, engineered, and manufactured by Henry Ford himself.

Well, not exactly himself. The tractor wasn't the product of the Henry Ford of Model T and Model A fame. It was the Henry Ford who was just an average mechanic but who was seized on by an unscrupulous capitalist who saw the name as a way to make money without producing a product to match it. And farmers who bought the inferior machines—not even imitations of Ford craftsmanship, just junk on wheels—were stuck with one of the priciest and most useless investments they would ever make.

It doesn't matter if the story is true; the situation was typical. Junk tractors were being peddled by unscrupulous exploiters. And the very people who were least able to afford fraud were the most frequent victims—farmers.

The Truth, the Whole Truth

For once, government did something right. On July 15, 1919, the Nebraska legislature made a law requiring that any tractor sold in Nebraska had to be tested and passed on by a panel of three University engineers. Okay, you say, that's just Nebraska. Well, it was more than just Nebraska.

Nebraska is a major agricultural state and a big tractor market, one not to be ignored by any serious manufacturer. And farmers, dealers, and governments in other states accepted the standards and evaluations of the Nebraska tractor testing facility so effectively, that if you wanted to sell a tractor in this country, you just about had to submit that machine to the rigorous testing of the Nebraska testing facility in Lincoln.

And what's more, no advertiser could use any part of a test evaluation without printing the whole thing. You couldn't talk about what a great puller your tractor was and ignore the fact that the blasted thing had to be repaired every hour on the hour. It was there in black and white—and it was *all* there in black and white.

Nebraska Tractor Test #1 was conducted from March 31 to April 9, 1920, on a Waterloo Boy Model N, and the tests continue to this day. As a lad, I occasionally passed by the testing facility on North 33rd Street on the University of Nebraska's ag campus and wondered what that weird device was being hauled behind a tractor on the concrete oval. Or maybe pushing the tractor, I was never sure. Year after year, decade after decade, the tractors ground their way around that track and underwent the indignities of having their sinew and soul strained, prodded, and examined for power, efficiency, reliability.

And the reports were published, an invaluable resource for international agriculture. These days I read the Nebraska Tractor Test reports because I am an old tractor enthusiast. So tests meant for farmers seventy-five years ago are still useful and valuable to a large public today. That's a pretty good investment.

The value of those tests is being questioned today. Manufacturers are pretty reliable, after all, and there are other state and federal agencies that serve as watchdogs against fraud. And these days it's best for a politician to cut a program, no matter how efficient and useful, and send 37¢ back to the taxpayer so he can say, hey, he cut taxes!!

Gone, But Not Forgotten

Thing is, the Nebraska tractor testing facility is probably on its last legs. A band of diehards is fighting to keep the testing facility alive, however. If nothing else, it will serve as a tribute to the tractors that passed through the laboratory's gauntlet over the years. Even if tractor testing is eliminated as a Nebraska state program, the facility will wind up as a tractor museum, a place where we can remember the successes and failures of a remarkable transition in agriculture.

As an enthusiast for agriculture, I lament the impending passing of the Nebraska test lab; as an old tractor lover, I applaud and anticipate its new life as a museum.

Chapter 19

Adieu, Fair Woodpecker— Roger Knew You Well

I told the first part of my adventures with the 1937 Allis-Chalmers WC tractor I labeled "The Woodpecker" in my book *Busted Tractors and Rusty Knuckles*. However, for those of you who weren't in your American literature class the day that book was discussed, I am a baby-faced beginner when it comes to tractor mechanicking (which is the way I like to spell the word when I use it to describe the religion as opposed to the occupation.)

Infected by the Old Iron Bug

About seven years ago, having never so much as changed the oil in an internal-combustion engine, I got the old iron bug, and I got it bad. My passion for old tractors progressed from virtual noninterest one July to a consuming pathology the next.

Somewhere along the line an old buddy, Dan Selden, took me to what gearheads call a "boneyard," a salvage yard for old tractors. Stromp's Dump, near Spalding, Nebraska, is where I met Jim Stromp, proprietor, good friend, and something of an ag machine nut himself.

Well, Jim and I got along well from the beginning. I bought some tractors from him, and some parts, and once, during some hot negotiations, I bargained him out of a wrecked WC tractor he didn't even know he had. Someone had painted the name "Silent Orville" on the gas tank, and it was pretty much a parts tractor. I intended to dismantle it somewhere along the line. You know, when I got to it.

Utter Ignorance

It took me several years to rebuild my first Allis WC, and I took quite a ribbing from my friends here in town about my utter ignorance of engines, transmissions, anything at all involved with mechanical devices more complicated than a toothpick.

Finally, in a snit, I issued a pronouncement at Eric's Tavern that when I got this wreck to running, I would drive it up to town, sit it outside the door of the tavern with the engine running, and the friends who had stuck with me would join me in drinking cheap champagne and listening to that engine run while the others gnashed their teeth. (I think it was on that occasion that Eric recommended that I not buy the champagne quite yet since the stuff only has a shelf life of three years!)

Jim Throws Down the Gauntlet

Well, the day came. I did rebuild that wreck, and it did run, and I did drive it to town, and I did invite my friends, and we did sit there drinking champagne and listening to the old girl, bedecked with black and orange crepe paper and banners, running cheerfully outside the open tavern door. I was wearing orange overalls. It was a grand day.

But at some point, Jim, one of the guests, stood with his glass—to offer a toast of congratulations, I thought. But he slapped me across the face with this gauntlet: "Rog, you may have gotten that tractor running, but you'll never get Silent Orville running."

What else could I do? A little over a year later, there was another champagne reception. And there was the newly renamed Roaring Orv, purring at the curb outside Eric's Tavern. I was disappointed that Jim Stromp wasn't there, since the whole thing was his idea.

And then there was a loud, low rumble. Dannebrog's main street went dark, and up rolled Jim's big, ugly hauling truck, loaded down with the most incredible wad of rust, tin, rubber, and kindling I had ever seen. The mess was barely discernible as a tractor.

"What's that junk twisted around it?" I gasped.

"A two-row cornpicker," someone sputtered.

Pointing to the trees grown up through the wreckage and the dead wood woven over and within it, I mumbled, "Looks more like a wood-pecker to me." Thus, its new name—The Woodpecker.

It Will Never Run!

Jim got down out of his truck, pointed to the wreckage on his truck, now surrounded by two-thirds of the population of Dannebrog, and said, "Rog, you may have gotten that first tractor running. And you may have gotten Roaring Orville running . . . But *you will never get this thing running!*"

Two years, hundreds of hours, piles of dollars, gallons of blood, and a heart attack later, The Woodpecker ran into town under its own power, flanked by Roaring Orville, Sweet Allis (my first love), and a half dozen other Persian-Orange beauties in a stunning diamond formation, driven by men and women all in orange, one of them is Dave Mowitz, the venerable machinery editor of *Successful Farming* magazine and the patron saint of tractor restoration. The spectacle was stunning.

My book, *Busted Tractors and Rusty Knuckles*, is a daily journal of my adventures and horrors in rebuilding The Woodpecker, and so it pretty much ends right there with the champagne reception.

The Woodpecker's Story Continues

And now there is more to the story. Early on in my tractor work, Linda asked me what I intended to do with a tractor I was working on when I finished. Well, I was stumped, because I'd never thought about that. I was pretty much done with them once I got them running. That's why I got them—to make them run. I hadn't given a thought to what happened after that. As far as I was concerned, once they ran and we had the party up at the tavern, the fun was all out of them.

As a result, thirty-five Allis-Chalmers WCs have been dragged onto this place in various states of destruction, and some have gone through substantial change, even improvement, but not one has ever left.

Well, folks, that is about to change. The Woodpecker is about to change hands. And for a good cause.

Some folks who love old tractors are in the process of putting together a new tractor museum on the agricultural campus of the University of Nebraska at the site of the historic Nebraska tractor test facility. And they need money to get this thing under way. So, The Woodpecker, probably the best documented tractor of all time, is going on the block. She will be the prize for a raffle designed to raise money for the museum.

She isn't restored. My work on her was anything but professional. The welding is pretty sloppy. I see that some of the soldering on the radiator is already coming loose. She comes complete with dents and scrapes. But she's a good old girl, and she was rescued from total defeat with loving hands.

And so we held a raffle drawing for this good cause: Get yourself a fine old tractor, give her a good home, and watch Linda smile like she's never smiled before when we haul that thing out of the yard. And don't mind the sticky stuff on the front pedestal. It's champagne. And Linda says to tell you that, if you want, you can even have the cornpicker.

Screams of Glee

The new museum sold raffle tickets for the year, making several thousand dollars, money that would go into restoration of other, more classic tractors. And although I was hospitalized at the time, with the help of good ol' Dave "Da Mojo" Mowitz, I helped pull the winning ticket.

There were some tense moments: Before we drew the winner for The Woodpecker, we drew some tickets for some of my books. The prize-winners were in California, Oregon, Alabama, Michigan . . . Uh, what happens if the winner of this tractor is in Maine? How are we going to get the thing transported? I mean, jeez, it's easy enough to mail a book, but a tractor?!

Then by long distance, with Dave's hand in the basket, we drew the winning ticket. And as such things seem to go, there was poetic irony aplenty. The Woodpecker was won by a woman in Plattsmouth, Nebraska, within easy driving distance of the state fair in Lincoln.

And here's the tough part for those who bought dozens of tickets, many months in advance: she had bought her winning ticket—*one* ticket—the morning of the drawing. When I called her to tell her she had one of the most famous Allis-Chalmers WCs in the world in exchange for the purchase of a one-dollar ticket, as I awaited her screams of glee, she said, "Uh . . . does it run?"

Sometimes the gods can be cruel.

As it turned out, I was gone when Jeffie Gravert came to our place to haul The Woodpecker away to the state fair, the new Nebraska Tractor Museum, and to her newfound fame. And as it turned out, Lovely Linda cried as The Woodpecker left the place.

See? Women *do* have hearts!

Chapter 20

Lessons From Tool School

I'd never admit it to Linda, of course, but I have way more tools in my shop than I need. I have open-end wrenches and box-end wrenches, metric and good ol' American regular. I have stubbies and extra-long, offsets, ratchets, crescents, sockets, and extra-deep sockets.

I have pipe wrenches, pin wrenches, and Allen wrenches. And then there are screwdrivers, hammers, pullers, gauges, priers—all that other stuff I just *had* to have to do things *right*.

What *Real* Mechanics Have

An uneasiness haunts my tool-drenched smugness, however. A few years ago I took a magneto over to the regional mag artist, a man famous for his uncanny ability to figure out and repair those mysterious devices. He hefted my afflicted magneto in his hands, peered intently at it, sniffed it, and then said, "Let's go over to the shop and take a look at her." Oh boy! A chance to get a look at a *real* mechanic's shop.

His shop building was clearly once an auto garage that lost its function when cars got too wide and too long to fit in it. At the back there was a wooden bench, with a rich patina of several decades of dirt and oil, under a single window and a naked lightbulb hanging from its wire. I presumed he must be one of those "operating room" mechanics who keeps his tools all neatly put away in drawers because only a couple items could be seen on the workbench. (My own inclination is more toward the "hide and seek" system.)

"Hand me my wrench," he told me. All I could see by way of a wrench was a battered crescent with a broken and rewelded handle, which I figured wouldn't be good for much except holding open the pages of a tech manual.

"Uh, which wrench?" I asked.

"Well, *the* wrench!" he snorted, pointing to the pathetic tool I had just dismissed.

And that, I found, was pretty much the way the morning went. There weren't any secret drawers or cupboards for his tools. It was a matter of *the* hammer, *the* screwdriver, *the* wrench. And the magneto I hadn't been able to fix with my full array of every tool known to Sears, Snap-On, Mack, Harbor Freight, and J. C. Whitney, he fixed with *the* hammer, *the* screwdriver, and *the* wrench.

Tried Hard to Understand

Which is not to say the experience left me any less enthusiastic about acquiring more tools. No, my tools are not simply functional devices with which I fix things. They are things of beauty in and of themselves. I can sit in my shop for hours, just cleaning and admiring my tools. I don't need to apply those lovely items to a single tightening or loosening. I am perfectly happy just knowing they are mine.

And that somewhere, someone is inventing and making more of them. It's not as if new problems are being invented for which we need new solutions. No, there are new tools, but the problems are pretty much the same old nuts, bolts, and screws.

I know what you're thinking: The last time you tried to repair the washing machine, you found that the thing is held together by curious little screws with little holes in the top the shape of the star on your Christmas tree (after the dog knocked it over two years ago and broke off one of the spikes).

The thing is, you're not *supposed* to have a tool to take those off because 1) the manufacturer figures you'll hurt yourself and sue them if you ever get inside that thing, and 2) they'd rather you hire their guy who *does* have the tool to get in there and pay him $75 an hour to pull out the sock that sneaked into the drive mechanism.

No, I'm talking about new screwdrivers to drive the same old screws. Ones with screw holders and turnable handles and little flashlights built right into them. Sockets with thinner walls, tighter grips, better steel, built-in alarms so you can find them when they roll under the workbench. Hammers with plastic heads, brass heads, pointy heads, round heads, square heads, with fiberglass handles, extra-short handles, extra-long handles, off-set handles . . .

And I will buy them all, at least one of each. Why? Because I *need* them, that's why.

Of course I shared none of this with my magneto mechanic. His philosophy toward tools is clearly different than mine. I tried to understand him, as I stood there watching him test my mag with a device he had made out of a piece of PVC pipe and an old spark plug, but I got nowhere. I tried to imagine what it would be like to have one wrench, and only one wrench for, oh, thirty or forty years. My mind went blank. The mere thought threw a circuit breaker somewhere in my brain.

Ah Yes, the Ultimate Instrument

In an effort, however, to make conversation and perhaps get some insight into this thought process so alien to mine, I said, "Dale, you know, they need to invent some sort of device a mechanic could use as a clamp, probe, fast weld, quick bolt, washer, shim, clip, cleaner, holder, grabber, hooker, electrical contact, scraper, and scratcher. Something with just the right rigidity and just the right flexibility, something not too expensive, maybe even disposable. Totally adjustable for length and size, strong but light and workable; something completely portable, compatible with every make of automobile or tractor—maybe even Linda's washing machine. Something . . . "

Dale handed me my magneto, repaired and ready to go, and said, "They invented it a long time ago, Rog. In fact, I just used it to fix up that mag of yours."

And he handed me a piece of baling wire.

Chapter 21

Dad's Tools

It's raining and cold. A good day to be in the shop. I am cleaning and putting away tools. Since I am not much of a mechanic, this undemanding task is usually my greatest pleasure. Nothing stuck, no mechanical problems, no expenses in cleaning and putting away tools! I have ZZ Top on the stereo. There are no demands . . . just clean and put away tools.

But I am not a happy mechanic. I'm not unhappy either. I'm just not happy. I'm—well, troubled, or uneasy, or something.

New Life for Old Tools

The thing is, all my life I have watched my dad in his shop. He could fix anything—cars, faucets, electrical switches, lawn mowers. Me, I never fixed anything until fairly recently, too late to profit from Dad's wisdom. I was the mechanical illiterate, son of the guy who could do anything. Isn't that the way it always goes?

Dad got mad when I used his screwdrivers for chisels. Or his chisels for screwdrivers. I never put his tools back where they belonged. I love Dad, but I never really appreciated what he did and what he knew.

I once told him I wanted to fix a chair I loved, and he said, "Take a little bit . . . " And I interrupted, "A little bit of what?" That ignorant response has become a legend in our family: Evidence of my stupidity before the man who knew everything.

Dad is no longer able to work in his shop. He's nearing ninety years old and has had some health problems. The folks will probably be moving soon to a retirement apartment. The last time I was at his house, he took me to his shop and told me to take what I wanted. He would never again be able to use his tools, fix what needed fixing. He waved broadly across his shop. "Take whatever you want."

On one hand, I hoped that meant he felt I now understand what tools mean. And that I would treat them, and him, with respect, that I would use them well. On the other hand, it meant he was done. No more polka music, no more sawdust, no more grinding, no more drilling, no more breaking loose stuck things, the ultimate task of the shade-tree mechanic. A huge part of Dad's life was gone.

It was almost scary, approaching those tools that had been off-limits to me for so long. I couldn't imagine holding them, yet taking them. Dad urged me on. Take the worn brushes and tired drill. Empty the rack of Craftsman wrenches. Did I want the brass hammer he made while he was working at the ammunition plant during the war? No sparks . . . Woodworking—was I interested in woodworking?

Passing on the Baton

Now I am in my shop more than 100 miles away, going through the boxes of Dad's tools, integrating them into my shop. Now those beautiful tools, so long an object of veneration and dread, are mine.

Tears run down my face—in my shop, of all places! Am I worthy of the worn screwdrivers, battered hammers, tired wrenches? Probably not. I have clear evidence that in some ways that I have become a better mechanic than Dad. I know a lot of things he doesn't know. And yes, he still knows a lot of things that I don't. But he has passed on the baton—his tools. Now they are mine. My dad's tools.

I put Dad's washers in with my washers. I throw away a jar of air gun darts; I have no idea why he had air gun darts. I add his big washers to my big washers, his pipe wrenches to my pipe wrenches. Curiously, and inexplicably, it is when I come across a jar labeled "common pins" that I finally can go no further. "Common pins." I stop the sorting. I put the little jar aside, intending to take it back to the house when I turn off the lights and close the door. I have no idea why. Maybe because I think of our family as "common pins." Maybe because I love the poetry of Dad's label on that jar—"common pins."

Measure Up to the Task

I leave the shop, for the first time in my life locking it as I leave and go back to the house. Tool thieves should be tarred and feathered anyway, but now . . . I go to our bedroom and put the little jar of pins on a shelf that serves us as a kind of ancestral altar.

"Common pins." Dad's tools are now mine, and I will never quite measure up to the task. His tools are nothing special—pretty ordinary actually. But now they are mine and I will never take one in my hands without thinking of all the times I saw them in Dad's hands, or carefully arranged on the board behind his workbench.

Common pins: I don't know why, but that seems to sum it all up pretty well. Common pins.

Author's afternote: Dad died September 30, 2000. And he did it with the style he showed most of his life. In his last hours he made us all laugh, told Mom he loved her, and flirted with a nurse.

This very day I was in the shop and picked up a small hammer with Dad's inevitable, inescapable trademark—a handle painted red. I smiled, chuckled, and wondered what the Old Man would think about my lovely shop where I actually do real mechanicking. And in honor of that grand old guy—pounded loose some corrosion inside a manifold.

Chapter 22

Old Tools, New Ideas

I'm in the process of unpacking my bags after a visit to Chicago and the National Hardware Show, the biggest exposition in the world of nuts, bolts, shovels, hoes, hammers, pliers, drill bits, lawn mowers, faucets, welding rod, and so far as I can tell anything else that's made out of wood, plastic, metal, or secret goo.

Machinery Editor Dave Mowitz has been telling me about this event for years, stressing the incredible vision of tools and hardware as far as you can see in every direction in a room big enough to hold Nebraska's entire corn crop for any one year. And that's just new designs for hammers and screwdrivers.

Then you go to another room that looks like a hangar for B-1 bombers and again, it's tools and hardware as far as you can see in every direction. And that's just plumber's washers.

Okay, maybe I'm exaggerating a little, but it is an astonishing exhibition, and the real exaggeration is the suggestion that any normal human being who is not an Olympic sprinter could possibly cover half of it in the four days the show goes on.

I saw a lot of terrific new tools in my four-day marathon walk up and down those aisles, but as is so often the case in such experiences, the real lessons took a couple days to soak in.

Impression #1: Someone once said man is a *tool-using* animal, but then when it was noticed that there are plenty other tool-using critters, that was revised to a *tool-making* animal. But then someone spotted some of those too. I think it was Tim Allen, the humorist, who observed that man is a *tool-borrowing* animal. Long ago I figured that some men (me, for example) are *tool-breaking* and *tool-losing* animals. The Chicago Hardware show convinces me that we are *tool-loving* people.

Impression #2: Nothing is ever finished. Did you notice that reference to "new designs" for hammers and screwdrivers? Those two tools should be just about the oldest in our toolboxes—they were used to build the pyramids and erect Stonehenge. Shouldn't we have the design pretty well down by now?

Well, according to about 10,000 tool companies, we don't. We need angled shanks, milled shanks, treated points, weighted heads, composition handles, ergonomic curves . . . It's amazing. Wait until you see them. You won't even know they are screwdrivers and hammers.

Impression #3: Nothing is simple. You may think burning a burger on a Saturday evening on your patio is about as basic as you can get: fire + meat = food. Not according to the world's hardware folks. You need pokers, jabbers, turners, twisters, skewers, basters, handlers, gauges, controls, cutters, lighters . . . You simply cannot imagine how inadequate you are if you just take a bunch of charcoal, light it with a match, and toss a meat patty onto a grid. You are, well, Paleolithic.

Impression #4: The human mind is incredibly inventive. I would've loved to have had an expense account that let me buy one of everything on display, put them together, and contemplate man's remarkable ingenuity. Take mousetraps. I listened to explanations of mousetraps (plastic, metal, glass, big, little, humane, vengeful, ergonomic) that left me slack-jawed and glassy-eyed.

And feeling about as inadequate with my old-fashioned wire-and-wood three-for-a-dollar traps I buy up at Kerry's Grocery as I now feel about that ridiculously primitive metal box I've been thinking of as a barbecue grill the past couple years.

Impression #5: If you haven't figured it out by now, for all my joshing above, I really am in awe of the dynamics and vitality of our tools and hardware. I think it's exciting that people are thinking, and inventing, and trying things out, and that other people are interested in what the inventors are doing, and buying the tools, and giving them a chance. I'm a man, after all. I love tools!

I came back from the Chicago show more confident than ever that the real engineers, designers, geniuses, thinkers, and hustlers in this world are folks working in their kitchens and shops, garages, and basements who stop while doing some ordinary chore and think—as lightbulbs flash on right above their heads—"Know what? I think I can do this better."

And more often than you might think, they are absolutely right.

Impression #6: Never underestimate the little guy. The biggest names in the tool business started with one man in a little shop with a good idea. Those little guys are still out there, still thinking, still putting things together, still excited about new ideas about tools.

And God bless 'em.

Chapter 23

Tractor Togetherness

Lovely Linda and I keep our marriage fresh and lively by finding things we can do together. For example, we go dancing every week. I go on Fridays, she goes on Saturdays. Just kidding.

We go to doctor appointments together, meet at the accountant's office to sign our income tax return together, sometimes even wave at each other as she heads toward town to buy groceries and I come back into the yard from a job where I have earned just a touch less money than she will spend on groceries.

Well, all that is going to change now. We are a modern family and we have an open marriage—I have Allis-Chalmers WC tractors and now she (it makes me feel dirty just saying it) has her John Deere B.

Linda has always been partial to green, she says, but she kept this little infidelity hidden from me. She looked at my Allises, smiled, and said they were very nice, all the while lying in her lovely way and fantasizing about a John Deere.

I'll spare you the details. It was almost by accident that not one, but four John Deere Bs—all without tires, most without wheels, all minus carburetors, magnetos, and other trivialities—were unceremoniously dumped in our yard. All I know is that I was doing a favor for a friend, receiving and storing one John Deere B. Maybe two.

Before I knew it, there were four of them, apparently multiplying on the truck even as they were being delivered. So, since there were clearly spare tractors, and of the very kind Linda has always wanted, she now has two JD Bs: one for restoration, one for parts.

Simplifies Gift Giving

Even while I was receiving the ridicule of all my friends in town, the glaring green spots standing like beacons among the Persian Orange, I did what I could to find a bright side to the situation. For one thing, I will never again have to wonder what to get Linda for Valentine's Day, her birthday, our anniversary, Mother's Day, Christmas, and all the other myriad female-generated occasions for the men in their lives to buy them something. Never again will I have to ponder how much to spend on flowers to apologize for whatever my current sin might be (misdeeds, I might note, that I can't even identify but nonetheless spring immediately to compensate for).

No, henceforth, a trip to Stromp's salvage yard, or Hilder AGCO Implement, or a quick telephone call to CT Farm and Country will be all I need to make myself a hero to Linda and her new love.

For Valentine's Day, a magneto might be just the trick:
> *You're the spark plug of my heart,*
> *Without you my engine is missing a part;*
> *You're still the girl whom I admire,*
> *So turn the crank and let 'er fire.*

I think a new tire might be an appropriate gift for Mother's Day:
> *Your love rolls on like this new tire,*
> *Never sticking in mud or mire;*
> *When times get tough, we don't care*
> *If you seem now and then to lose a little air.*

And for anniversaries, well, here's where I kind of ran out of air myself. I looked through all the books about love and marriage in the

Dannebrog library but couldn't find a single bit of advice about what tractor part is most appropriate for which anniversary. I therefore propose the following for those of you who follow in my tracks and buy a spouse a tractor by way of bolstering up your nuptials:

1st Anniversary: This being traditionally a paper anniversary, a set of gaskets seems particularly fitting.

2nd Anniversary: Welding gloves (cloth).

3rd Anniversary: First-aid kit to make up for not buying leather gloves last year.

4th Anniversary: His and her socket sets.

5th Anniversary: 10 quarts of scented crankcase oil.

6th Anniversary: A romantic evening eating popcorn, drinking strawberry daiquiris and watching engine rebuild videos; one for Allis, one for John Deere.

7th Anniversary: A luxury trip to the tractor show of your spouse's choice.

8th Anniversary: A complete new trousseau in the color of your spouse's tractor.

9th Anniversary: Fifty shares of stock in AGCO, Allis, Case, Ford, etc.

10th Anniversary: An exchange of paints and decal sets (a genuine display of love and respect).

11th Anniversary: Well, you get the idea.

They who restore together . . .

Frankly, I'm not sure a marriage based on two passions so utterly at odds can last more than ten years, but who knows? Linda is a Catholic; I'm a Protestant. She is Czech; I'm German. Most troublesome, she's a woman; I'm a man.

But we have now survived for eighteen years. So if we can walk that narrow and troubled path and maintain a happy marriage, maybe we can overcome this most recent of tensions straining our marriage. Hers is green, and mine is orange—but they're both old tractors!

Chapter 24

The *Real* Green Monster

One of my many virtues—right up there with my enormous modesty, in fact—is that when I make a mistake, I own up to it. And here I am, about to do some major owning up.

I have written in a couple dozen articles and books that while my passion is for Allis-Chalmers tractors, especially the venerable Model WC, I am color blind when it comes to old tractors. I love 'em all. And anything I might say otherwise is only in jest.

Well, I was wrong. Now I want a constitutional amendment requiring a three-day waiting period for the purchase of an assault tractor, and I am ready to start circulating a petition to that effect right here and now. Surely we can agree that the constitutional guarantee to bear tractors in a well-regulated restoration obsession does *not* include John Deere tractors.

So, what brought about these negative feelings in the heart of this otherwise genial and easygoing old coot? Plenty, that's what. Let me just give you a couple examples. One late winter day not long ago I was walking home from town with the mail, just strolling along the left side of a gravel street at the edge of town, minding my own business, when I was run down from behind by a tractor.

Sure, I heard him coming, but jeez, he had the whole road and I was way off on the left shoulder and the last thing in the world I thought this green monster would do is come clear across the road to collect me and throw me down into the ditch with a shattered left hand and broken ribs.

As I lay there looking up at the snarling beast looming over me, I wasn't even surprised. Sure, I was surprised to be run down from behind. Sure I was surprised it was a tractor. But I wasn't even remotely surprised by the color. Green. John Deere green.

Really Got Ribbed

The folks in town had their share of fun with my discomfort. John Carter said it was probably just another case of me chasing vehicles and biting at tires. The Blakes from across the road said it was my own fault for not wearing my slow-moving-vehicle emblem, and gave me an orange vest with the distinctive, bright orange triangle so it wouldn't happen again. Linda asked the farmer to put the tractor down since once a Deere tastes blood, you can never trust it again.

I got anonymous mail blaring "Nothing Runs (You Down) Like a Deere." And the EMTs who picked the gravel and burrs out of my head laughed that they were probably there from the night before when I walked home from the tavern. A couple days after my mishap someone put up a sign at the site of the accident. Yep, "Deere Crossing."

But as humiliating and painful as that Deere encounter was, I was not ready to hold all John Deeres responsible for the misbehavior of this one bad example. In fact, when I learned of the availability of a nicely restored John Deere B, instead of volunteering to put the blasted thing out of its misery with a stick of dynamite, I offered to buy it from the owner for my Lovely Linda. Her father and grandfather had a John Deere B, and she often speaks of moments on the old farm, standing on the drawbar as one of the men in her family drove that old B out to the fields or around the farmyard. What a great Christmas gift that tractor would make, right?

Did its color bother me? I'll have to admit, that after being run down by one, folks in town could scare me into jumping behind a tree or into a culvert just by making sounds like a Johnny Popper, but no, good ol' Rog wasn't going to hold anything against a tractor just because it dang near killed him. From behind.

So I bought that tractor for Linda.

The gifting ceremony was a tender scene. Linda's father and mother came to our farm for the presentation. After some initial confusion (her exact words were: "A tractor?! For Christmas?! For me?! What were you thinking, Welsch?!") Linda graciously accepted her Green.

The tractor sat in the backyard where we could admire it for a couple days and then some storm warnings were issued for our area and I thought I better get it under cover to protect that pretty, new paint job.

It took me a little time and effort to get it started, and in doing so, I learned a small thing about starting John Deere Bs, namely, to wit, viz: You can pretty much figure on getting your right leg completely soaked with gas because JD Bs were built with this particular and peculiar feature a part of their apparent attraction.

Making an Entrance

Reeking of fuel, however, I got up on the seat and drove out of the yard and toward my shop. I had just rolled an Allis WC out to make room and it would be a good, safe place for Linda's new prize. I opened the doors, pushed some things aside, jumped back into the seat, noted approaching storm clouds, and patted myself on the back for my good sense and good timing. And I drove through the doors into my shop.

Well, maybe that isn't exactly the best description of what I did because I took the doors with me. And a substantial part of the entire front of my shop. You see, the rear wheels of a JD B can be moved in and out according to the width of your rows, and the wheels on this one were set as far in as possible, leaving the axles sticking out to the side about a foot on each side. But not visible from the driver's seat.

I pretty much tore off both sides of my shop entry, knocked the doors into the shop, which then brought down the overhead sill on the door, with lots of sheetrock, two-by-fours, and insulation, pretty much right onto the top of my head.

All of which left me about $\frac{2}{100}$s of a second to learn how to use a hand clutch before I went through the back of the shop, leaving nothing much but two walls and a roof, unless they fell down too, in which case I wouldn't even have that.

As Linda and I were surveying the wreckage, she told me sweetly that her dad had told her at the tractor presentation that he did the same thing the first time he drove his JD B into his garage. So, if he knew perfectly well what was about to happen, why didn't he tell *me*?! Eventually I had to tow Linda's Deere out of the shop. It wouldn't start. And hasn't started since. It just sits there now in the lean-to, being green and mean. I passed a log chain around the rear axle and a big ash tree just in case it takes a notion to jump out at me and run over me sometime when I'm out in the yard. There's not a doubt in my mind that it is capable of that kind of misbehavior.

Today, as I gathered up a hammer, nails, screws, and lumber, I looked wistfully at my collection of Allises. And just as I turned back to the miserable job of rebuilding my shop, I could have sworn I heard a soft but metallic voice whisper from one of my Persian-Orange beauties, "I told you so."

Chapter 25

The Making of a John Deere Expert

In a previous column I told you about getting a John Deere B for wife Linda for a Christmas present—an improvement, she says, over the time I bought her a shotgun. But not much of one. At any rate, now that we have had this malicious beast for almost three months, I'm pretty much an expert on this model of John Deere, about the same as I am an expert on the Allis-Chalmers Model WC, in fact. I even got it started once.

There are signs that Linda's tractor was not reassembled with total care and precision, but I hope to work some of those problems out at another time if I can ever get it started again. For one thing, the clutch doesn't work worth a darn; I don't know how many times and how hard I pushed on that blasted pedal and still couldn't get it into gear without a terrible grinding of gears. My left foot is still sore.

Moreover, with just a little investigation I think I've figured out why it won't start, let alone run. Dick Day, my buddy who restored the tractor and sold it to me (he should run for Congress; he has all the qualifications), was either in too much of a hurry or maybe thought he could scrounge enough parts to make two tractors out of one. Thing is, when he reassembled this machine, he left off two of the cylinders. Unless they're somewhere else, because all I can find is two.

And even then, I tried to check the ignition setup on the thing but Dick just hung up on me when I asked him what the firing order is. Maybe one of you readers who knows something about green machines can give me some help on this.

The John Deere is going to take some getting used to, no doubt about it. I tried to use it with my buzzsaw but had one heck of a time getting my big old Allis belt to fit on that skinny little belt pulley. And who designed these things anyway? You can't get at the starter switch or choke when the belt is on the pulley!

Good Advice Is Helpful

My John Deere pals up in town have been very helpful—more than usual, in fact. I think it's because I'm now a member of the Green Brotherhood. They usually just give me a bad time whenever I ask them about my tractor problems, but this time when I described my woes at getting the thing running, they showered me with good advice.

Kenny Porath pointed out one possible problem that might account for the reluctance of Linda's new machine to run: The gas line had been mistakenly hooked up from the carburetor to the gas tank rather than from the gas tank to the carburetor. He said that he could fix that up for me but would have to charge me for two hours labor, no cost on the parts. What a guy!

Dennis Adams suggested that I dismantle the fuel pump and put a rebuild kit into it, which I am going to try this very weekend. He even had a spare fuel pump kit that he very reluctantly let me have for $40.

Dan Selden chimed in that his dad had pretty much the same problem with a John Deere B but in his case the problem turned out to be the water pump. And darned if he didn't have a complete (and very rare, he says) overhaul kit for a John Deere B water pump, which he let me have for another $40.

Melvin Nelson got to looking around Linda's tractor and just happened to notice that it was missing its crank. Well, in no time at all he was looking through the drawers in his shop and just happened to find a like-new John Deere B crank, which he dang near *gave* to me for, well—$40. Funny how that works out, huh?

The bottom line of this little story is that an old tractor is an old tractor. If you know anything at all about one, you pretty much are set up to work with any of them. Don't be shy if you haven't worked with an engine before. It's all plain and obvious once you get into them and look them over.

. . . But Where Do You Get That?

You're a Deere man and want to get started with Allis WCs like mine? No problem at all. All you need is a set of Allis socket wrenches. I'm sure Dennis or Dan can help you out with a little thing like that. And if you are missing something (it's pretty hard to find an Allis WC with an original gas gauge, for example) just ask around town. You're certain to find some good buddy who is ready and willing to help you out. And in all probability it won't cost you much more than, well, uh—$40.

Speak of the devil, here's Al Schmitt coming into my drive at this very minute with that muffler oil he said he would round up for me. And he said he could get it for me at a good price. With pals like mine, it doesn't take long to get an old tractor up and running darn near like new. And I'm willing to bet that given half a chance, they'd do the same for you.

Chapter 26

Lists

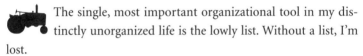 The single, most important organizational tool in my distinctly unorganized life is the lowly list. Without a list, I'm lost.

I suppose I could take on the philosophy of my buddy, Dennis "Bondo" Adams, who says that he starts every morning making a list of what he needs to do that day, and when he loses the list, he knows he's done. But what I usually do is make another list. And then I lose that one. A couple times a month the lists all resurface, and then I am confronted by twenty-six lists, all with different items, all in different order, many of them requiring me to do things I've already done. Or decided not to do.

Once I tried to take care of this problem by making a list of my lists. Household, shop, outdoor, work, travel, Linda's requests, and uh, all the things that don't fit on any of the other lists. Didn't work. I lost the list list.

Important Items Like "Frmbǵǵl"

If that were the only problem, I could live with it. But even when I find my list for the day or week or month, my troubles aren't over. I would estimate that about once per list I get ready to set off on the day's adventures and find that along with "service tractor," "haul garbage," "fenceposts for Linda," and "gravel at mailbox," there is an item reading something like "Frmbggl."

Frmbggl? What's Frmbggl? It must be important or I wouldn't have put it on the list. But if it was important enough to write down, why can't I remember what it means? I'll do the gravel, fenceposts, tractor, and garbage, but my whole day will be ruined worrying about Frmbggl. Since I never figure it out, and the world seems to continue spinning, I suppose it wasn't all that important to begin with. But man, I can't help but wonder.

The satisfaction of a list is crossing things off, of course. And like finishing a crossword puzzle, the ultimate joy is crossing off the last item. Conversely then, nothing can be more annoying than going out to haul the garbage and along the way, carrying out the aluminum for recycling, bringing in another bag of dog food, and tightening the wires on the clothesline, only to find that you forgot to write them down on the day's list! Oh no! Four jobs done—but only one item crossed off the list! The zest just seems to go out of life.

List It for All It's Worth

Pretty much in the same category of lifetime letdowns are jobs like my annual, dirty, long task of shredding the high grass and brush in the pasture around our house to cut down on the fire hazard it presents. Taking the blade or drawbar off the tractor is enough of a job, but then mounting the shredder is always tough on my muscles and disposition. Then I sharpen the blade; another two hours down.

Then I bounce around in the dust and heat for days, stopping for repairs, moving big and little hazards, lifting the shredder to avoid chopping dirt, lowering it to keep the grass as short as possible. Three days later, I put everything away and cross off my list "shredding." One item, one word: shredding. Three days. One item. It just doesn't seem fair.

I've solved that problem by adding to my daily lists items such as "Brush teeth." "Put on shoes." "Eat lunch." Do 'em, cross 'em off the list. Got a lot done today.

Lists Somehow Grow on Their Own

The solution is not simply to add things to lists, however. One of the reasons I think I lose my lists is that I have taken to hiding them. If I don't hide them, I find that my lists grow pretty much on their own, for all the world like a thistle that is a cute little rosette one day and a towering old-growth redwood the next.

What's this? I don't remember putting down "Clean attic" on today's list. Is this my writing on the list for tomorrow where it says "Rebuild fence around the daylilies?" And how about the mysterious item under Things To Do Next Month: "Don't forget wife's birthday again this year—and no, a new shotgun won't do. Think roses, chocolates, a movie, and dinner, Big Boy. Or else." Did I put that there? I don't think so.

But I better not cross it off until I'm darned sure I have it done. And it might be a good idea to move that particular item to the top of the list.

Chapter 27

Mr. Rustoration Answer Man Ponders the Mystery of Magnetos

One of the most common questions coming into my Mr. Rustoration Answer Man mailbox is " Mr. Rustoration Answer Man, how do you deal with old tractor electrical system problems?"

In my book *Old Tractors and the Men Who Love Them*, I wrote that one of the reasons I love my Allis-Chalmers WCs is that there isn't much of an electrical system to them—just four wires, one going from the distributor cap to each of the four spark plugs. Of course there's more to it than that.

And as time has passed we have come to enjoy technological progress—which is to say, more things to go wrong. Later-model tractors came along with things that generated heat, sparks and potentially fatal charges—batteries, generators, lights, fuses, switches, ammeters, and spouses, for example.

Thus we discover the first rule of working with antique tractor electrical systems:

Rule #1: Don't work with old tractor electrical systems.

I once watched Big Don Hochstetler up in town check the ignition on my tractor, Sweet Allis. He pulled the wire from each spark plug and held it far enough away so he could analyze the color, sound, and inensity of the spark. At one point he dropped the wire, jumped back from the engine, and shook his hand vigorously.

"Get bit?" I asked.

"Nope," he responded. "I was too fast for it."

Since that moment I have been cautious about checking sparks on my own. Now that I think about it, it wasn't since that moment. My understanding that electricity is for people who don't think it will do next time what it did last time came unto me when my country cousin Dick took me, a city boy, with him to get the cows and said, "Hey, Rogie, wanna hear the craziest sound you ever heard?"

"Sure," I said, clueless.

"Pee on that," he said, pointing to a single wire running around the pasture on thin little rods. I did, and indeed I did hear the craziest sound I'd ever heard: It was me, screaming at the top of my urban lungs. My education was enriched by that experience and since then I haven't touched anything that looks even remotely as if it might have electricity in it, let alone pee on it.

On the other hand, I recently asked my buddy Dan Selden if he thought the mag on my workbench was any good. He picked it up, looked it over, rolled it around, flipped the shaft over a couple times, yelped enthusiastically, and said, "Yep, it's good."

And I learned something from that too:

Rule #2: It's okay to let someone else fool around with something that looks like it might have electricity in it.

Actually, I have recently gotten information that there may even be times when it's appropriate to take the bull by the horns yourself. I recently suffered what is daintily described as a "coronary episode." There was some talk during my hospital visit of "defibrillation." That's what they do on television when the doctor yells, "Clear!" and places two pads on some unfortunate's chest. There is a violent zap and the afflicted person's body leaps into the air, pretty much like I did when I showed disrespect for Uncle Fred's electric fence.

Fortunately, I wound up not having to go through that, but more importantly, a Nebraska doctor who loves old tractors wrote me suggesting that instead of paying all that money for a hospital procedure, I could simply throttle back my Allis to about 400 rpm, unhook the wire from the third spark plug, lick my fingers, and grasp the spark plug nipple with my left hand and the end of the spark wire with the right. A jolt would come along about 100 times a minute—a fairly decent pulse, when you think about it. If that didn't set my heartbeat in order, it would probably kill me, but in either case, I wouldn't have to worry about the hospital bill. Obviously this doctor understands Rule #2 as well as I do.

Now, where was I? Oh, yes. Briefly, a magneto system works like this: The engine turns a timing gear or belt somewhere along the line somehow, which turns a little shaft generating electricity by some means or another and releasing it variously in synchronizations with the pistons going up and down by some force by some means or another, so that the spark plugs fire in some order or another, just at the right time somehow to ignite the fuel, if everything goes right.

Confused? Right. If you are confused, then you got the idea.

Rule #3: If you try to understand an electrical system, you're in for disappointment.

What is the difference between a magneto and a generator, you ask? And how about an alternator? Well, that's a question I can answer: A generator differs from a magneto in that "generator" is found in the index under "G" while "magneto" is found under "M." "Alternator" is under "W" for "way too complicated for you to fool around with."

A vehicle's distributor has a little rotor in it that goes around and hits connections that go to each spark plug, and when the points separate, a surge of power that is stored up in the capacitor goes running down the wire and makes the spark.

Huh? Surely I must have that wrong. Well, yes, it does make sense that the power should go down the wire when the connection is *made* by the points rather than *broken* but we're talking electricity here, not sense.

No, the wires aren't hollow so the electricity can run inside like a hose: Electricity moves through wires by, uh, doing something else, something that water doesn't do. It releases loose ions and electrons and watts, or maybe it's amps, and they do something inside the wire that doesn't involve water, and electricity moves even though nothing like water is really moving. Except that maybe water in the mag or distributor can cause problems.

Actually, now that I think of it:

Rule #4: Everything in an electrical system should be listed under "W" in the index.

You say your tech manual says to turn the mag rotor clockwise to time your engine but you don't know if that means clockwise looking at the mag from the distributor end or the mag end of the rotor? Well, I can understand how that could be a problem. Here, let me hand that mag to my pal Dan. He'll check it out.

Rule #5: Get a buddy like Dan.

I know what you're thinking. "Rog, when you work on a tractor, it always winds up running just fine, so obviously you have figured out how to deal with these complications. So what's your secret?"

Please, please, please. We are not talking nuclear physics or brain surgery here, and it's not a secret. For all my kidding around, the bottom line is, a little common sense, some resourceful thinking, and a lot of patience can get you through any electrical problem.

I know no magneto magic, nor do I possess exotic tools and circuitry testing devices that give me an edge, nor was I born with an innate talent for ohms, watts, volts, zaps, and zowies. Tractor electrical problems are easily solved, and believe me, if I have figured it out, you can too.

Nor am I the kind of guy who's going to keep this information to himself. I have been a teacher all my life; I am still excited by the free exchange of information that characterizes our wonderful hobby.

Have a problem with your electrical system? Can't figure it out? No problem. Call Melvin Nelson. He knows all about tractor electrical systems.

That's what I do. Call Melvin. How does *he* do it? He has magneto magic, exotic tools, testing devices, and inborn talent. And he keeps the information to himself.

Rule #6: Reread Rule #1.

Chapter 28

R. Welsch, Retired

Somewhere, I think it was in the *Guinness Book of World Records*, I read about a guy in Ohio who bought two antique tractor wheels and neither one was rusted out. I hear the *Guinness* people are pretty careful about checking the authenticity of their records, but I have my doubts about that one.

I've never seen *one* antique tractor wheel that wasn't rusted out in all my life, let alone two at the same time. Or any two tires that had more than a ¼-inch of tread left on them, or that weren't flat, or leaking noxious fluids. Just doesn't happen. Ask anyone who's ever had anything to do with old iron. Doesn't happen.

A Quick Education

I remember with some tenderness the first time I took a wheel and tire off of my Allis WC. One of the first things I learned about old Allises is that squarish spokes are more than likely old iron-lug wheels that have been cut off and retrofitted with rims for rubber, and round spokes are probably wheels actually manufactured for rubber.

Okay, Sweet Allis, my first love, had squarish spokes; I had picked up a salvage tractor with round rims. So I figured, if I just switched 'em around, I'd have a much more authentic item, right?

And with just that kind of sweet innocence that comes from igno-rance, I jacked up the left rear of Sweet Allis and loosened the lug nuts. (One of the very few occasions in my now-long experience when one lug didn't stick as if welded in place—probably because that wheel and tire had another, even bigger surprise in store for me.) The last lug came loose easily and I tugged at the gigantic tire to pull the assembly from the axle. Boy, is this ever going well, I thought to myself.

It was approximately one $\frac{1}{57}$ of a second after the last tug that I learned that tractor tires are more often than not filled with liquid to give them weight and thus bite on the tread.

Now, understand this if you are not familiar with tractor stuff: A back wheel on a tractor, even a little Allis G or Farmall Cub, is heavy enough as it is. It's not something you would want to fall over on you. But fill it with liquid, it is in league with the anchor of an aircraft carrier, in both weight and grace.

The tire of my favorite tractors, the Allis-Chalmers WC, is not one of those monsters you see in the fields today, but I suppose it weighs 200 pounds or so. Fill it with liquid and you have something with—well, Lovely Linda provides the appropriate metaphor—the weight and grace of *me*!

So, unlatched from the axle, that wheel and tire, therefore, began a slow tilt outward and I reached forward to stop it and hold it upright. It took only the slightest contact for me to figure out I wasn't going to stop it and it wasn't going to stay upright and the very best plan for me was to throw myself as violently as I possibly could out of the way of that monstrous weight or I was going to be the shop equivalent of road-kill opossum.

Later that day I raised the tire back to vertical with the front-end loader on another tractor. I mean things are not simply clumsy; we're dealing with major tonnage. I got the wheels shuffled okay, but mostly—I learned about tractor tires.

Noxious Mystery Liquid

What is the liquid in those tires? You can't just use water because it would freeze and provide a ride about as comfortable as solid iron. Oil would be too expensive.

As far as I can tell, they fill tractor tires with toxic nuclear wastes. How do I know that? Well, for one thing it eats through iron like I chew through a prime rib. For another, wherever this tire liquid leaks on the ground, you can pretty much count on having something as sterile as Death Valley because nothing is going to grow there ever again for all eternity. This tractor stuff is deadly.

I have an Allis-Chalmers WC tractor "on steel," which is a tractor guy's way of saying that instead of rubber tires it has iron wheels with solid iron lugs. These are pointy studs that look like something off a medieval war machine.

I thought it would be fun once to drive this super-iron tractor up to town and show it off to some friends. I figured out that I could drive all the way to town in the ditch so I wouldn't damage the paving on the highway. I know this may sound a bit overly cautious, but even I could figure out that if you put a ton and a half of iron on little iron points, you are going to do some damage to whatever happens to pass under those wheels!

When I got to town and turned onto the gravel road, I realized exactly what kind of damage that could be: Those lugs chewed up the streets in such a way that I knew I was going to be in real trouble with the town maintenance man if I proceeded another six feet toward Main Street. Old timers later told me that the thing to do is to get the tractor up to some speed so that the lugs "skip along the top of the ground" and don't bite in.

Yeah, right: "Skip along the top of the ground . . ." Even before I got to the gravel road in town I learned that the last thing I wanted in my life was to get that machine up to a speed that would allow it to "skip along the top of the ground."

No Rubber, No Padding

Again, for those of you who are not familiar with old tractors, unlike automobiles a tractor doesn't have shock absorbers or springs. Everything between the bottom of the rear tire and the driver's butt is iron. There is no padding on the seat, often no spring to the pedestal on which the seat is bolted. On most of my Allis WCs, the only "give" at all between the ground and my tailbone is the flexibility of the rubber tire. Take away the rubber tire and there is no give whatsoever. On the way up to town that day, I felt shudder up my spinal column every rock, beer can, and cigar butt lying in that ditch.

In the whirlpool bath that night as I soothed my aching back after that half-mile trip on an iron-shod Allis, I pondered those noble men of the soil who tilled millions of acres of American soil on tractors like mine. Maybe they got them up to speed so they, uh, "skipped along the top of the ground." Uh-huh. Oh yeah. You bet.

Somewhere along the line these past ten years I learned the bad news that buying brand new tractor tires is something Donald Trump or Bill Gates might be able to afford, but not your run-of-the-mill amateur tractor restorer. And then I got the *good* news that I could get combine or center-pivot irrigation tower tires that would fit on my old Allis rims much cheaper.

Since I never use my tractors for real farm work (I live in fear that if they ever get started dragging old tractors out of sheds to put them back to work, they just might consider doing the same thing to old professors), cheaper, less substantial tires would do just fine for my purposes.

The one possible problem with these substitute tires is that while the tires fit my rims all right, they are larger overall than standard tractor tires. Now, the problem I worry about with these larger tires on the drive wheels is, when I am going down I-80 in road gear, how can I be sure I'm not exceeding the 75-mph speed limit? Several physicists have given me formulas to help me figure out my velocity but what with the wind in my hair and the bugs in my teeth, making slide-rule calculations while driving simply has not worked out well for me. Think I'll stick to gravel roads. Then I should be okay, right?

Mind the Tread

One last note on tires for those of you considering entering the old tractor world: There is a frontwards and a backwards to rear tractor tires. And even if *you* don't know the difference, or care, you can bet everyone else in town will.

The day I turned the Allis WC dubbed The Woodpecker over to the Nebraska Tractor Museum to be raffled off, I had to get wheels and tires on it. I was dreadfully busy (about to head out of town) so I was careless and didn't pay attention to the orientation of the tread. And fate being what it is, of course I got the tires on backwards. A fact that everyone at the state fair, the site of the raffle drawing, was quick to point out to me.

I knew I was going to be in trouble for this tractorial gaffe, so, thinking fast (which is something I can do when the clear penalty is going to be personal humiliation) I came up with an explanation. The tires are not on backwards at all, I explained. I, uh, I bought this tractor originally as, er, yeah, as Iraqi army surplus. And they put all their tires on backwards. For the best traction when they jam them into reverse.

That seemed to work, and that's pretty much all I know about tractor wheels and tires.

Chapter 29

Accessories

Ask any woman: The secret to the perfect ensemble is proper and creative accessorizing. Yes, the classic basic black sheath is always the ultimate haute couture chic, but it's your earrings, shoes, necklace, and fingernail polish that truly make the fashion statement. At least that's the way I've always looked at it.

Okay, actually that's not the way I've always looked at it. Mostly, my fashion statements run more toward the right kind of carpenter pencil in the bib pocket of my overalls, a jaunty red kerchief in my back pocket, and just a *soupçon* of manure on my boots, but you get the idea. Accessories, that's where it's at.

All too often this basic rule of fashion is ignored by the tractor restorer, and at his own peril I might add. How many times have I had to click my tongue and shake my head at some poor sap who thinks his Cockshutt 30 is pretty to the point of being perfect, never for a moment thinking about the painful omission of the requisite Prince Albert tobacco can over the open exhaust stack!

I remember with embarrassment (for the tractor owner) the time I was judging the famous Limbo, Nebraska, restoration competition. I was going down the line of tractors, neatly outfitted and polished. (I was neatly outfitted and polished, that is.) The contestants were trailing along behind, nervously biting their lips and watching me make my notes at each stop. I rather imagine they all figured I would drop the winner's laurel wreath over the radiator cap of a perfectly done-up 1937 Allis-Chalmers WC unstyled tractor, which everyone knows is my favorite machine in this world anyway.

The tractor was indeed a beauty. Everything was authentic. The spring on the throttle rod to the carburetor had broken loose, as is proper, and the steering column wobbled in the top solid bearing block, just as it should on any decent Allis WC. The gearshift lever flailed madly, apparently broken completely free from the gearbox, and a ¾-inch bolt was in the drawbar—a sign of good taste in tractor accessorizing.

I lifted the winner's wreath and was about to drop it on the winning Allis, proclaiming it the victor, the best of the nearly 2,000 tractors I had looked at that morning when, on some kind of whim, I opened the toolbox on the back left fender.

And there it was. Or more precisely, there it wasn't. Somehow the restorer of this otherwise perfect machine had forgotten to add the appropriate accessories to this vital feature of his tractor. Not only was there no mouse nest in the box (you won't believe this!) there was also no broken spark plug or rusty monkey wrench with the battered back end. (I know what you're saying: What was this guy thinking?!)

Since that terrible moment I have found again and again that restorers will spend thousands of hours and dollars rebuilding motors and transmissions, polishing paint jobs, and finding just the right rubber for a restoration, and then inexplicably forget to wind a wad of baling wire around the drawbar, thus totally destroying any historical accuracy in their work.

More Blatant Omissions

The list goes on: A Case CC at the Ennui, Iowa, show without a couple chains wrapped around the drawbar; a Minneapolis-Moline Twin-City Universal Z at the Lake Awgowan Show without the necessary stick "gas gauge" hanging from the steering column; a Massey-Harris 101 at the big show in Dull Center, Wyoming, without a "necking knob" on the steering wheel; an entire row of six—*six!*—McCormick-Deering Farmall Ms at the Painun, Missouri, Tractor Show without a single Vise-Grip pliers serving as a replacement for a lost or broken knob; three Allis-Chalmers Cs, two WCs, and one B at the Confiscatory, Texas, exhibition last year without one ear broken off a cooling system drain plug.

"Oh, the humanity!" I wanted to scream. "Whatever happened to authenticity?! What's next? A Ford 9N without a mud dauber's nest under the sheet metal?! An International 300 without the Torque Amplifier lever snapped off? Am I the only one who cares about historical accuracy these days?!"

Well, maybe I'm just being obsessive. Linda will tell you I've always been a perfectionist. The same thing happens when I see some Hollywood type wearing overalls . . . with all four side buttons done up! Yeah, right, like any real overall wearer ever did that, except maybe for a funeral!

Or the time in some television show whose title I have mercifully forgotten when in one scene the "farmer"(!) drove up to the gate, got out and opened it up, drove through, got out and closed it again, got back in the truck and drove off—instead of telling his wife to get out and open it while he drove through! Spoiled the whole show for me. Not to mention that it took me almost a month to retrain Linda.

But come on, people. Let's start paying more attention to these details. They're small, but they're important.

Chapter 30

Naming Names

 Don't listen to the poets. They're all wrong. "What's in a name?" they ask. Well, I can tell you. A lot, that's what.

The process of naming a tractor is, for the old iron enthusiast, right up there with naming a new child. In fact, now that I think about it, there are a lot more people with kids than there are with old tractors so actually, it's quite a bit more important. But don't tell Linda I told you that, okay?

I didn't know a thing about tractors when Dave Ratliff gave me my 1937 Allis-Chalmers WC, but it was only a matter of a couple of weeks of living with her before I determined that she was a she, and labeled her "Sweet Allis."

In one of the very first articles I wrote about old iron, I pointed out that the serious antique tractor collector should always *name* his acquisitions rather than numbering them, because while "Red Betty" gives out only information like name, rank, and serial number, "Ol' Number 22" is more like spilling troop strength to the enemy, if you catch my drift.

Now I have worked on "The Woodpecker," "Roaring Orv," "The Stromsberger," "The Fanta-sizer," and "Dale's Folly," to name just a few, monikers that just seemed to spring naturally from the very nature of the machine itself. Some tractors, on the other hand, just don't want names. My faithful and beloved International 300 has never been anything but "The International." The C is "the C" and the WD is "the WD," the Cub is "the Cub" and . . . well, you get the idea.

I have noted before that Linda's John Deere B was instantly dubbed by her "Simply Irresistible," because I remarked to her (while desperately trying to convince her I got a good deal on it) that it was simply—well, no doubt about it—*gorgeous*. She thought of the Robert Palmer song, the one with the gorgeous swaying babes in the background, and edited the name, on the spot, to Simply Irresistible. Thinking of the line in that song, "You'll wonder where the money went . . ." I instantly concurred.

There are generic names like "Johnny Popper," "Minnie-Mo," that sort of thing, and the utter wackiness of the designations assigned by manufacturers: "880," "300," "WD-45," "UH," none of which, so far as I can tell, have anything to do with anything. They're just letters and numbers picked out of the air, I guess.

Inspired Dubbing

As I do so often, I turned to my friends at the Antique Tractor Internet Services website to see if they had any theories about how tractor lovers name their machines. They didn't let me down. Dean A. Van Peursam, along with mountains of good advice on how to get Linda's JD B running, echoed the experience of many tractor namers, explaining that the names he calls his tractors depend a lot on how serious the injuries are that they've just inflicted on him.

Rick Kiser wrote that he once had a Ford 8N that he named (and I have cleaned this up a little bit) "Bellybutton," because everyone has one.

Tractor veteran Phil Auten has a theme to his tractor naming. His biggest, a Farmall M, is named "Bluto," the Allis RC was "Popeye" because it did most of the work, and the Farmall C was "Wimpy" because, well, because it was, compared to the other two. It was only natural then that an Allis B was dubbed "Olive Oyl" and the Cub, "Swee' Pea."

Robert Thompson also used the comic pages for inspiration, naming his '56 Case Terratrac 600G "Old Snort," because "it did" and because "it's kind of purposeful looking too, like Snort, the old boar hog in the Snuffy Smith comic strip."

Pop culture seems, in fact, to offer up a lot of name sources for tractor nuts. Charlie Hill named his D-14 "Uncle Allis" in tribute to the Beatles' "Uncle Albert." Dave Merchant has his "'Enery the H," after the hit song by Herman's Hermits. Dave also has "Maggie" (an F-12 with magneto problems), a "haze blue van, about the color of the old CSX 'Stealth' paint scheme . . . and it produces an excellent smoke screen."

Ken Knierim writes that his $200 Case DV that came home in several loads and is still in pieces is called "Basket Case." Larry Sikes has "Old Bark" ("Listen to it run and you will understand"), "Pusher" ("used to push/shove/force everything"), "Old John" ("he's just the old guy"), "Little Red" ("because he is"), "Clunk" ("because he does"), "Fred" ("don't know why, he just seems like a Fred"), and "Grunt" ("because he does all the grunt work").

Creates Even More Character

Bill Boyd's 1944 Farmall A is as old as he is, so it's "Grandpa," and his 1972 Massey Ferguson 165D is "kept in a doorless shed that is so small, when you park it, you can only see the rear end . . . so it is called 'Big Butt.'"

But for my taste, the prizes for tractor naming go to Gilbert Schwartz, who has labeled his Allis WC "Teddy" ("short for the rough-riding SOB,"); Frank Wardley, who calls his old blue and gray Ford 850 "Old Blew"; and best of all, my most favorite, the now forgotten soul who told me he named his antique tractor "Lost Dutchman," because like the mine of the same name, it has so much gold sunk into it and gone forever.

And they say the art of poetry is dead! Whoever said that must have been the same guy who said "What's in a name?"

_____

Chapter 31

Online Auctions: Why Would Anyone Want to Go?

I'm about as stodgy an old goat as they come. I like old stuff and I like the old ways of doing things. Which is to say, I have come to accept newfangled notions like e-mail, the Web, home pages, even computers slowly, even reluctantly.

Nowhere has that been truer than with auctions. Why, half the fun of an auction is watching other people buy really dumb stuff at prices that are way too high while I acquire unrecognized values at bargain-basement prices. Not to mention saving the family pride by outbidding that idiot Chuck Stooge who thought I'd let him walk away with that genuine reproduction of an authentic Rembrandt in the lime-green plastic frame.

Church-Lady Lunches

And there's the lunch served up by the ladies over at the Lutheran church, and a chance to talk with old friends you hardly see at all any-more except at auctions. At a farm auction you get to see how badly ol' Ralph took care of his tools. And hey, isn't that your breaker bar he borrowed two years ago in that box of broken wrenches?

If you have a really good auctioneer at work, why, it's almost like a concert of traditional music. And a good auctioneer usually has the best new jokes from around the country, and if he's from the area, he knows everyone, how to get the top dollar out of them, how to pick on the cheapskates, how to play that crowd like a fine piano.

Why on earth would anyone want to go to an auction on the Web?

I did. Because I had some tractor instruction manuals I wanted to sell. And, frankly, I didn't know how else to sell them. As always, I was a little uneasy about venturing into a world I don't understand at all. Mostly because I presumed I'd make a fool of myself pretty much like I do every time I ask daughter Antonia anything at all about my computer or the Web. "Da-a-a-ad," she says in four syllables. "Sometimes you're *so . . . slow!*")

But, fearing the worst, I went to the Antique Tractor Information Site auction page (www.OldIronAuction.com) and I came out of the experience feeling pretty darn good. Even I, the "slow" one, had no trouble figuring out how to put my manuals up for auction. And for several weeks I followed the bidding (a lot slower than Colonel Chuck and Tom Wieck run their auctions) but no less interesting. Especially as I saw the bids go beyond the minimum price and well beyond what I thought I would get for the books.

At the end of the period I had chosen for bids to be open (four or five weeks) I got the checks for the books, exchanged some friendly conversation with the buyers, sent along the books, and paid the modest commission percentage of the selling price to the website. I even had some cyberconversation with the auctioneer. Just like home.

Well, not quite. I didn't get indigestion from that sagging lemon meringue pie I got at the last outdoor auction I went to. And I didn't get dreadful sunburn like I did over at Olson's sale. Or stand in the rain and mud and catch a cold I couldn't get rid of for the better part of a month while trying to push my truck out of the muck like I did at Stanowyck's sale two years ago.

The Value of Online Auctions

In fact, my experience with the ATIS auction was so positive, I went to two book auctions on the computer in my office and bought two antique books for Linda for Christmas. And it was during these purchases that I realized the real advantage, and maybe a disadvantage, of online auctions. I didn't have to travel to fifteen auctions in miserable weather, hoping that the "box of old books" listed on the sale bill might have something—anything—Linda might like.

Nope, I could look precisely for what I had in mind, had plenty of time to think about how much I wanted to spend, and didn't have to worry about bidding $87.50 on a lamp made out of a cream can when I waved a fly away from my ear.

The disadvantage is that I also know I'll never buy a box of miscellaneous hardware and find a set of Snap-On eight-point sockets buried in the bottom. Okay, so I'll still have to go to farm auctions, mostly for recreation and to pick up things I don't really need at prices I really can't afford, but when I have something to sell, or something specific I am looking for—I'll meet you on the Web.

Before . . .

. . . After.

Chapter 32

Blast It!

My affection for working on old tractors started on the inside and worked its way back out to the skin. The first thing I ever did with an old Allis-Chalmers WC tractor was rebuild the engine; I am now working on developing some skills at welding and finishing the sheet metal, which means that I am having to become less and less the mechanic, more and more the artist (pronounced "art-*teest*").

Right now, I'm working on my skills at sandblasting, and what an epiphany that has been! One of the most enjoyable parts of engine work for me has been that process that many mechanics find absolutely odious, cleaning parts. I simply don't know how to explain my pleasure at this task. I hate washing dishes. But just sitting at my workbench, picking away at carbon bits, dirty, greasy, ugly-bugglies is such a quiet, pleasant, harmless sort of activity that is best done on a rainy or snowy day when I can occasionally look out my window and just be glad to be alive and in my warm, comfortable shop.

I'm not quite as tickled with cleaning corroded manifolds, rusted camshafts, filthy blocks, or irretrievably caked oil pans. They're too big to be any fun. And the dirt doesn't just chip or brush off, even with a power tool. That dirt is permanent. Or at least it seems to be permanent. At least it *used* to seem permanent.

Blasting Basics

But it isn't. A sandblaster will take it off. Like magic. And not just take off the dirt but leave that part as shiny as it was when it was brand new. After a year or so of working with my very low-tech, inexpensive sandblasting outfit however, I have learned enough about the process that I figure I can pass along some basic information to you in the unlikely event that you know even less than I do. (In which case, you should be pretty embarrassed, if not downright ashamed.)

Basically, what a sandblaster does is combine a very fast jet of air from your compressor (and now you have an excuse to buy that big compressor you've been wanting) with something solid—like sand—which is then directed against whatever it is that you want cleaned. Then the nasty little grits of sand, moving at the speed of an F-16, literally wear off dirt, rust, and eventually the actual substance of the part. And if you're not careful, your overalls, the welding cable you didn't notice under the part you are cleaning, and the back of your left hand, if you forgot to put on your blasting gloves.

For example, I have found it to be a very bad idea to try to eat a peanut butter sandwich while sandblasting unless your family doctor has suggested that you could use more fiber in your diet. A lot more fiber.

It is also a bad idea to do your sandblasting in the family garage without closing the car windows. Similarly, I recommend against sandblasting parts upwind from the Little Lady's clothesline when she has sheets hanging up to dry, or worse yet, your overalls.

Aim Carefully

Whether you're using glass beads, silica sand, or walnut hulls, they are going to come back to haunt you if you're not careful about where all that stuff goes once it leaves your blasting gun, hits the metal you are cleaning, and wafts downwind. You also don't want to blast even upstream from cooling pies, sunbathers, or a charcoal grill full of steaks. Especially filets. The risk is just too much.

Always consider the appropriate setting and timing for sandblasting. Do not sandblast, for example, in the same room in which later that day you intend to apply the final coat of paint on a restored tractor. Do not attempt to sandblast parts over the kitchen sink. Also, do not sandblast in the nude, or even in your pajamas. Although this seems to be a problem that pretty much takes care of itself after the first mistake.

In fact, a large part of successful sandblasting is good protective equipment. When sandblasting it is a good idea—a *very* good idea—to wear gloves, although there is always the built-in advantage of getting your fingernails cleaned at the same time you are removing rust from an old PTO shaft.

Be sure to wear good, tight goggles, or better yet, a full face mask when sandblasting, because otherwise you're going to be kept awake by the sound of your eyelids scraping across your eyeballs all night. This is especially true if you wear contact lenses. Get blasting sand under those babies and it's like trying to read around rocks.

One word of caution from bitter experience: While wearing a sandblasting hood, do not attempt to make a withdrawal from your savings account, even in the local bank where everyone knows you by your first name and should know by now what an idiot you are. Also, do not to walk past three nervous black Labrador retrievers with that sandblasting hood on.

I know that showing up in elbow-length gloves, an apron, and a full-head hood just might reinforce the impression in town or with your wife Precious Moments that you really are working and that you really *are* a mechanic (not to mention that it makes you feel just a little bit like an astronaut) but believe me, you're going to be surprised at how many people can misinterpret the intentions of a man in a mask and hood.

True Grit

I once did some sandblasting while wearing shorts. Then I walked to town for a beer. This was not a good idea. I would prefer not to go into the details right now, and believe me, you would prefer that too, but let me just say that I walked funny for a long time thereafter. And never sandblasted again in my shorts.

No matter what you do wear (stout pants, overalls, flannel shirt, leather apron) be sure to shake everything off (shirt, pants, socks, dainties) well before you throw those clothes into the washing machine. As it is, when you finish with your shower that night, you're going to be able to shovel out the bottom of the shower stall and fill in that two-acre washout on the north side of the house. Believe me, the lady who does your laundry has already had just about all she can take fishing washers, bolts, cotter pins, live bait, and magnetos out of the bottom of her washer; she's not going to be at all happy about finding three-quarters of a yard of drift sand down there too.

The materials you use in your sandblasting equipment must be chosen with care. There are lots of different kinds of abrasives you can blow through that air machine of yours and each one offers a different degree of severity in what and how much it takes off the part you are cleaning. There are soft abrasives made from nutshells or wood granules that barely take the dew off a lily; on the other hand, there are grits that can convert an aluminum carburetor bowl into a thimble in about three seconds if you're not careful. Which is to say, be careful.

No matter what material you use for a grit, no matter what air pressure you use to blow it onto the part you are cleaning, let me offer one little bit of advice, and I bring this to you from my heart: Whatever else you do, don't hold the part you are sandblasting in your lap while you are doing the work. Especially if you are wearing shorts. (As I said, I did this. Want to see my scars?)

An Ounce of Prevention

If you use sand directly from your child's sandbox, or for that matter from your own, be sure to carefully sift out all the cat poop. And don't tell me there isn't any cat poop in there because if there is a cat within fifty miles of your house, and believe me there *is* a cat within fifty miles of your house (in fact, I'm betting there is a cat watching you from the bushes at this very moment, just waiting to poop in your sandbox), there *is* cat poop in your sandbox.

I am not trying to tell you what to do here. I'm not that kind of guy. What I am trying to do is save you from making a lot of mistakes that I made. That way you can move on to making mistakes of your own and tell me about them so I don't make them—not that I've shown that kind of good sense in the past. When you get right down to it, making mistakes in the shop is for me pretty much like that cat poop I was telling you about. It's going to be there, no matter what you think, no matter what you do . . . it's going to be there.

So let's be careful out there.

Chapter 33

Ol' Rog's Rustoration Resource Guide

Let's say you are in the middle of rebuilding a tractor magneto and all at once there is something you need. Perhaps only to ask a technical question or get some advice, but you need to dial up someone fast. And here you are, out in the shop, the phonebook is in the house, and besides, you don't want to waste a lot of time looking up numbers anyway.

What could be more handy, then, than a list of all the numbers you might need, tacked right up there on the wall next to the shop telephone, or glued onto the front page of the phone book, or under "Important Telephone Numbers" in the neat and careful filing system you use in your shop office.

Of course, everyone's specific needs will differ, but let this list (my particular list of important numbers) be a general guide for customizing your own. If you cut out this list, fill in the appropriate numbers, and post the form someplace where you can easily find it, your problems are over. No, don't bother to thank me. It's just another service of Ol' Rog.

Ol' Rog's Rustoration Resource Guide

Attorney:
> Divorce Attorney:
> Liability Attorney:

Bail Bondsman:

Bank:
> Loan Desk:
> Overdrafts:
> Repo Agent:

Bondo's Paint and Body Shop:

Burn Center:

Chiropractor:

Credit Card Customer Service Desks:
> Payment Extension Department:
> Lame Excuses Department:
> Loan Limits:
> Credit Services:

Environmental Protection Agency Appeals Office:

Eric's Drive-By Beer Delivery:

Family Counseling:

Fast Break Travel Bureau:

Fire Department:

Helpful Harry's Pawn Shop:

Hide-A-Lot Storage Units:

Hospital:
> Emergency Ward:
> Visitor's Services:

Industrial Laundry Supplies:

Insurance Company:
> Claims Department:
> Liability Claims:

Interior Redecorator:

Junk and Salvage Yards:

    Pick Up:

    Delivery:

Law Enforcement Offices:

    Bomb Squad:

    County Sheriff:

    City Police:

    State Patrol:

    FBI:

    IRS:

    Alcohol, Firearms, and Tobacco

        SWAT Team (Domestic Disturbance Division):

Medical Supplies (Wholesale Division):

Pizza Delivery:

Poison Center HOT LINE:

Psychological Therapy:

Sorrier Than You Can Imagine Flower Shop:

Tractor Restorer's Anonymous:

United Nations International Stuck Bolts Relief Station:

WOOF-TV Action News Hot Tip Line:

Wholesale Cleaning Supplies:

Of course, this listing is not complete and you will have your own additions to make, but you gotta admit, it's a start.

Chapter 34

Roger's First-Aid Kit Supplies

Not long ago, in a cardiac ward somewhere in America's heartland, a nurse was making her thirty-seventh futile attempt to find a vein in my arm into which she intended to place a ¾-inch plumbing faucet. Lovely Linda watched the process for a while before laconically, and accurately, noting, "Give him a butter knife and in three minutes you'll have all the blood you want."

Okay, so I'm a trifle accident prone. And yes, I'm a bleeder. Also a bruiser. And a breaker. And a burner. EMT schools could do worse than to have trainees just drop by when they see my shop lights on, because they'd be absolutely certain to find a rich variety of ordinary and unusual injuries for practice purposes. If not, they could just give me a butter knife, and in three minutes . . .

It shouldn't, therefore, be a surprise to anyone that one of the first things I did when I built my own shop ten years ago was to buy a large, industrial-grade first-aid kit, which I then tacked up in a prominent and easily reached place. And it wasn't one full day before I realized that industrial grade or not, the world of medical science hasn't kept up with me when it comes to self-inflicted wounds.

I have, therefore, begun to assemble my own shop medical kit. I realize that you probably have your own specialties when it comes to banging yourself up and will almost certainly need items specific to those needs. But let the list below provide a start for your own medical kit, and feel free to drop me a line about your own suggestions for my list. In the meanwhile, excuse me while I change the dressing on these burns.

The Roger Welsch Hopeless Klutz Shop Medical Kit

1) Hernia trusses in assorted sizes, for every part of your body, including eyeball hernias when you get that new *Sports Illustrated* swimsuit calendar.

2) Ice pack: Don't skimp on this one; a 50-pound potato sack should be just about right).

3) One (1) gross tetanus booster syringes.

4) Full-body gauze pads.

5) Sanitized hospital-grade duct tape.

6) Bulk antiseptic system: 60 gallons with electric pump; if you inflict cuts and abrasions on yourself like I do, a gravity feed antiseptic system just won't do the job.

7) Oxygen tanks: The tank from your gas welding outfit will do, but be sure you have the hoses straight and you are sucking on the oxygen hose, not the acetylene outlet. Especially if you smoke.

8) Bulk burn ointment: One 30-gallon tub is a minimum, but you may want to add another for backup if you do any welding.

9) Self-loading gurney: If your shop is more than thirty feet from your house, you may want to have a motorized version. You may be best off with a gurney made from a converted or double-duty engine hoist to save time before the EMTs arrive with their own equipment.

10) Crutches in assorted sizes and grades.

11) Surgical grade Vise-Grip pliers for removing splinters from various parts and sand, wood, bolts, or pistons from your eye.

12) One sterile winch for stuff stuck in you that the Vise-Grips won't pull out.

13) Eye rinse: 60 gallons or a fire hydrant will do (see item #11).

14) Two-by-fours for splints: Several hundred board feet should do.

15) Large mirror: This will allow you to see personal damage where you sat on that newly welded side rail. Note: while I do recommend a mirror, I strongly urge you *not* to include a magnifying glass in your medical kit. If you're in my league, all personal damage will be big enough to see, and you won't want to see it any closer.

16) Paint brushes: For applying ointments and disinfectant, but for larger wounds, a paint roller may be more appropriate.

17) Isopropyl alcohol: To prevent infection in external wounds.

18) Jack Daniels Green Label: To deaden pain from external wounds and to lift the internal spirit.

19) Mobile phone predialed to 911.

20) Viagra in a large, bulk container, with handy wall dispenser: This item may strike you as a peculiar feature for a list like this, but if you watch the television commercials for this particular medication, you will see that it apparently makes old people dance and sing, which is always a desirable condition in which to both enter and leave the shop, wounded or not.

And there you are. Stay healthy, and let me know how those bones set.

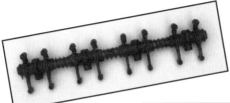

Rocker-arm
assembly
prior to restoration.

Rocker-arm
parts.

Rocker-arm
assembly
after restoration.

Rog wondering what went wrong.

Chapter 35

High-Tech Restoration

One of the wonderful ironies of restoring old tractors is that we modern mechanics are not restricted to the monkey wrenches, machinist's hammers, and scissors jacks the original owners had to struggle with while rebuilding an engine or adjusting rocker arm gaps. By now you know that one of the principal pleasures I take in my shop is not just *working* with tools but *holding* them, *looking* at them, *knowing* they are there . . .

And I don't just mean those lovely sockets, lithe breaker bars, and silky-handled pliers and wrenches, nor big, roaring, steaming compressors, welders, engine hoists, or cute little seal pullers.

Nope, I'm talking computers here. How's that for bringing together two worlds from just about as far apart as worlds can get? A 19-horse-power 1937 Allis-Chalmers WC tractor and a maxigigabyte, 12-billion-baud modem, hootin' tootin' Deskpro Compaq with a movie-quality wall-mount monitor screen!

Nor is that all I am throwing at you here. How about a Sony Digital Mavica MVC-FD73 Zoom 10X Quick Access FD Drive 2X camera? Yep, I am suggesting to you old-timey mechanics that there is a place in your antique tractor shop for all these things.

A Couple Possible Applications

One of the hardest things I've had to learn in my brief but meteoric mechanicking experience is to remember the order in which parts come out of or off of the tractor so they can be put back *in the same order* when it comes time to put the tractor back together. It's not all that easy. In the relatively simple, small rocker arm assembly of an Allis WC, for example, there are almost twenty-five parts, and they all have to be put together in *precisely* the same order in which they came apart.

If you are a novice like me, you may not even notice that there are exhaust valves and intake valves until you have taken them all off. And then it's too late. Believe me, if you put parts on backwards or in the wrong order . . . well, you don't want to put parts on backwards or in the wrong order.

I have tried to take notes as I have dismantled some tractor component or another. Doesn't work. For one thing, it's hard to know exactly what you should be writing down, or how: "The little thingie with the shiny knob on the end fell off before I had a chance to see exactly which end goes into the squarish hole first, but I think it is the non-shiny end." And see? You forgot to write down that the slotted side goes *up*! And since you're working up to your elbows in filthy grease anyway, your notes wind up well greased so that even if you could understand what you wrote down, you couldn't read it anyway.

And of course when you need the notes, you'll never find them.

Okay, I'm here to solve this problem: Your digital camera and computer are the keys. What you do is take a picture of the component you are about to work with before you take off the first bolt, nut, clip, or screw.

Then very carefully disassemble the unit. Slip each part off and lay it down immediately on a clean surface. When all parts have been removed and laid down in order, simply take another photo.

Clean, repair, replace, adjust the parts (whatever needs to be done), and then drag out your digital images. Either hold them on your monitor screen or if you have a printer that will print images, simply run off a copy or two for use at your workbench. *Using your digital photos as a*

Before . . .

. . . After.

Forensics detectives can use your photos to determine exactly how you came to be squashed under that John Deere wreckage.

guide, reassemble the unit. And there it is, precisely put together the way it was in the factory sixty-five years ago.

That is only one application of modern technology to the restoration of antique machinery. You can also use your digital camera and computer to record your accomplishments, such as "before" and "after" shots of your restorations.

Photos taken before a visit from your brother-in-law, and then again after, can help insurance companies determine losses.

I'd show you some more examples, but unfortunately earlier this morning Linda loaned my digital camera—to my brother-in-law. I'll get back to you on this.

Before visit from brother-in-law.

After visit from
brother-in-law.

Chapter 36

Start Me Up

I have written elsewhere that one of the most precious moments in a man's life—next to the birth of a first child, purchase of a first automobile, or first peek at a *Playboy* centerfold—is starting up a long-dead, laboriously rebuilt tractor.

In my case, I take years to tear down a tractor and rebuild it, and my joy is to take a total wreck, preferably with a stuck motor (cars have engines, tractors have motors; cars freeze up, tractors get stuck, for those of you who are new to the science), totally dismantle it, put it back together—and have it actually run again.

It's almost scary. I mean, wow, you've spent all this time, made 1,000 changes and adjustments, poured so much energy, money, time, and soul into this thing, and now here it sits, awaiting your command to rise and run. Will it? Now is the moment . . .

But, uh—how do you start it?

A rebuilt tractor is a *tight* tractor. There's a good chance that even if you have carefully torqued down rod cap nuts to precisely the correct foot-pound measurements, pre-oiled or greased bearings, pistons, rods, and lifters, left perfect clearances twixt rocker and valve stem—you're not going to be able to turn over that stiff engine by hand.

Moreover, if you've tinkered with the timing or governor, there is every chance in the world that crank is going to kick back and make about six death-dealing spins trying to break off your hand, smash your nose, and give you a head start on a sex-change operation.

There has to be a better way than grabbing that crank and reinflating that hernia you paid so much to repair three years ago. And there is. In fact, tractor restorers have come up with several techniques for that first start up.

Initiating Ignition

Perhaps the most commonly used method is that of dragging the rebuilt tractor up and down the road behind another tractor. This is always good for amusing the folks along the route as they watch the closest thing to a parade they have seen since the Fourth of July, for encouraging full employment of the road crews that will repair the damage you do to the gravel or pavement, and for generating reasons for a 1) celebration party or 2) bereavement wake since you are going to need at least one or two other guys to start a tractor with this technique. (Never ever involve a wife or daughter in this process! Don't even ask why. Take it from me, you just don't want to do that.)

Believe it or not, the towing technique is also good for your vocabulary and grooming. The sixth or seventh time the chain or tow strap comes unhooked or rolls under the front wheels, you will find yourself discovering words you thought you forgot long ago, words you haven't even thought of since your childhood when your father's 1937 Dodge slipped off the jack and tore a hole right through the back wall of the garage on its way to knocking down the table of potted flowers Mom had out back.

As for grooming, in the hour or two of towing, adjusting, towing, adjusting, towing it takes to get the tractor running, it will blow roughly six gallons of black oil up through the exhaust stack and back onto the driver, i.e., you. All this oil will add luster to your hair and skin, a luster in fact that could be there for weeks.

In the event that you do not have a length of road down which you can drag a ton and a half of dead iron, or if you should have a constitutional aversion to public humiliation, you may want to try an alternative starting system.

As always, when working with equipment, caution should be exercised. A couple bright young fellows around here once engineered a device that joined the power take-off axle from one tractor to the one they hoped to start. They used a small, light Allis-Chalmers C as their starting tractor and hooked the PTO shaft to the John Deere 8650 they were trying to start. By the time the shaft finally snapped off, that little C had been rolled over and over about 150 times. Neighbors were picking up parts and Persian-Orange sheet metal as far as two miles away for weeks.

Having learned a big lesson about PTO shafts and tractors, these boys next rigged up a big electric motor with a fitting that could be pushed onto the crank union at the front of the next tractor they worked on, thus saving a lot of work turning a hand crank. They were buried with a real nice service right here in the Dannebrog cemetery. And the St. Paul cemetery. And the Elba, Cotesfield, and Farwell cemeteries. Even the Nysted cemetery, as I recall.

It Takes a Team

After starting one of my iron lug-wheeled restorations with the towing method, hauling it up and down my own road down to the bottomlands and pretty much finishing up the plowing for the year and eradicating totally our mole problem, I got pretty uneasy about that system. Thing is, we were having carburetor and magneto adjustment problems, but we couldn't really make adjustments to get the tractor to run without having the tractor running.

So what we did was have my buddy Lunchbox drive the towing tractor while I steered the restoration machine. Woodrow ran alongside the tractor I was steering with a screwdriver and pliers, trying to adjust the engine as he ran sideways down a rough, graveled farm lane, about two and a half feet in front of those ferocious iron lugs and grinding wheels.

Right off, being a former professor and all, I could see some potential problems in this arrangement, like me having to deal with Woodrow's widow and seven children. I mean, Daisy probably would have been happy enough to see Woodrow turned into a gravely grease spot but feeding those kids would have been another problem for me altogether.

So, the next time I had a tractor ready to fire up (an unfortunate turn of phrase for a couple of examples I'd rather not talk about at this point) I knew I had to do something other than the Galloping Mechanic Method. Well, Allis WCs have dandy belt pulleys on the right sides of their frames. So I reasoned that if we put the restoration tractor nose to nose, a crossed belt looping together both pulleys, we could use the running WC to start the restoration. We arranged the tractors, started the runner, looped and crossed the belt so the engine was turning in the right direction, and eased up on the clutch of the restored machine.

It worked. In fact, it worked just fine. Yes, as always with a flailing, grabbing, jagged, working belt pulley, there is the adrenaline rush that comes with taking your life in your own hands, but the fact of the matter was—it worked. The three of us, Woodrow, Lunchbox and I, stood back and looked at each other, smiling. And just a little disappointed. We'd never had to deal with one of these start ups without there being plenty of stories about stupid mistakes, painful injuries, and close calls to stupid mistakes and painful injuries. Somehow success just seemed to take the fun out of it.

I have also heard of guys putting the rear of a rebuilt tractor up on stands and starting it by turning the back wheels. That sounds pretty much like an idea Woodrow and Lunchbox would come up with. As I recall, stories about this technique usually wind up with the tractor falling off the jackstands, exiting through the back of the shop, and finally stopping when they run out of gas after running through about sixteen different fences or coming to a halt after climbing up the back of a father-in-law's Lexus.

Electricity Shows Promise

I usually say that electricity is for sissies, but the truth is, I don't believe in electricity. I understand absolutely nothing about it and the only thing I mess with that I am absolutely ignorant of is women, and that's just plenty enough, thank you very much.

Now, don't get me wrong: There is promise in a tractor electrical system. There is battery acid to be spilled, polarities to reverse, motors to burn up, fuses to blow, shocks, jolts, volts and amps . . . more than enough to keep a guy like me busy for a long time. But when I have an electric starter tractor that won't start up, I still prefer the towing method.

I tow it up to town and let Al the Mechanic figure out what's wrong.

Rog with his
St. Valentine's Day valentine.

Chapter 37

Welding in the Fast Lane

If you've ever done any welding, you know that it really is fun melting metal and sticking things together, even if it can hurt really bad now and then. I recently acquired a MiG welding outfit (MiG = Multi-injury Gizmo) and got to playing around with it. It makes welding child's play. And you will understand that all the more if you'll just sit down sometime with a child, give the little tike two or three warm chocolate bars and a jar of jelly, and watch the action for a couple of hours.

I have actually done some functional welding in my shop. I made a battery box once that was only a little too small. And I have even fixed a few things around the house. I braised an Italian coin to the top of my corkscrew one time when I broke it off trying to open a bottle of wine that turned out to have a screw lid.

(And for those of you wiseacres who are going to make a fuss about how stupid I am because "to braise" is a method of cooking involving the crispy burning of the outside of the meat while "to braze" means to join together two pieces of metal with a third molten metal, well, you've never seen me work in the shop or cook over charcoal. The way I do them, both processes involve the joining of metals and the burning of flesh.)

Spicing Things Up

But there comes a time in Advanced Welding Techniques when the expert becomes downright playful with the torch, tossing it behind his back, welding blindfolded (and just closing his eyes and following the bead through his eyelids!), that kind of thing. The ordinary tasks of welding become everyday, and need a little spicing up.

Well, I have made myself a hero in my home and something of a landmark in the world of welding by solving even the most unlikely problems with my welding torch and new MiG unit *by making things for my loved ones!* I prefer the element of surprise; hearing in the ordinary conversation of the day my daughter, wife, or a friend mention something they need or want, I then sneak off to the shop to fill the gap.

But after a couple years of this, at even the slightest suggestion from someone that something is needed (a new prom dress, an embroidery hoop, a bookmark), I raise one finger, widen my eyes, and before I can even say it, the family chips in with "Think I'll go out to the shop and weld something up!"

Inline Skates

This first started a couple years ago when my daughter Antonia was moping around because all her friends had inline skates but she didn't. And I, noting that even the discount price for these toys was nearly $100, decided that I would just—*go out to the shop and weld something up!*

I was thoroughly pleased by my solution (a pair of inlines that cost almost nothing since I used scrap metal, and the visit to the emergency ward doesn't really count because that kind of burn could have happened eventually no matter what I was working on) and as I told Antonia, given a little time, those wheels will wear out round.

As it turned out, just about the time I brought the first skate into the house, Antonia decided she really wasn't interested at all in inline skating, so I wound up sending the sample to my other daughter, Joyce, in Seattle, who opted not to ask me to complete the second, since UPS charges something like $20 for a package weighing 30 pounds.

Valentine's Gift

It was perhaps a year later that my skills were next called to the front line, and this time in the name of romance. It was a couple days before St. Valentine's Day and as yet I had found nothing for Linda. I thought about my options: flowers wilt and are thrown out in a day or so, and next year you just have to buy more. I have found that while chocolates are always welcome, I then have to listen to months of complaints about what they do to hip padding.

So, I'm looking for something more permanent than flowers, less fattening than chocolates, but dripping with romance. A diamond? No, that's not it—*I think I'll go out to the shop and weld something up!* The result was a 40-pound, ½-inch steel heart, complete with initials on the top, opening up to reveal—*ta-da!*—it's plum packed full of jerky! And not the homemade kind, complete with hair and teeth. No, this was store-bought jerky, your high-class mesquite kind, and barbecue variety, and, for the exotic taste—*teriyaki!*

As you can imagine, Linda was so stunned, she cried like a baby and couldn't find the words to express her appreciation for almost a full week. She loves it so much, she has asked me to keep it out in the shop where it will remind me of how much I love her. I think that's why she said I should keep it out in the shop anyway.

The Perfect Tiara

It was not long after Valentine's Day that I caught Antonia moping around about her homecoming dance outfit. Okay, I have three daughters, so I have grown accustomed to the reality that they buy dresses for more than $100 that they will wear only once, while I buy overalls for $30 that I will be wearing for the next ten years. So, she knew she was going to buy a dress. And shoes. And a jacket. And probably a new car, since the old one clashes.

But (Dad's eyes brighten visibly even as she speaks) she has not been able to find just the perfect tiara! Exit Dad, stage right, out to the shop—*to weld something up!*

When she came home from school the next day, there it was, a splendid, perfectly regal tiara, all 16 pounds of it; not the sort of thing that is going to fall apart in a Nebraska spring wind or during a wild polka (or whatever it is kids dance these days). I'm not up on these things but everyone remarked that it made Antonia look like some fancy fashion model named Cindy Lou Who.

Unfortunately, being a careless kid, Antonia misplaced it just before the dance and didn't find it until after the senior prom. And actually, I was the one who found it, lying in the yard iron pile out behind the shop. No one can imagine how the heck it wound up out there.

There you have it. Who knows what's next? All I know is that your shop's welding equipment is no longer just for fun and profit: It is a surefire device for bringing the expert welder the gratitude and love of his entire family. And I'm sure Linda, Joyce, and Antonia would be the first to tell you that if they were in here, but well, I can see they are out there in the yard . . . Huh—looks for all the world like they are trying to build a fire up against the west side of the shop, right in that pile of brush and cardboard. Huh. Wonder what that's all about?!

Rog presenting Antonia
with a tiara.

Afterword

Well, there it is, a tidy collection of what I have done so far over the past few years for *Successful Farming* magazine's Ageless Iron. I hope you have enjoyed reading them half as much as I did writing them and spending the time in my shop acquiring the material. For all my joking, you know, I really do love the time I get in my shop, the work I do with old tractors, and the chances I get to talk with others who are afflicted by this terrible disease called Old Iron.

I'd love to have you all drop by and sit around the woodstove with me, talking carbs and mags, comparing tractor colors, but just as some people's businesses depend on folks dropping by, mine pretty much relies on folks *not* dropping by! But I hope you will continue reading my books and my columns in *Successful Farming*.

If you are so inclined, drop me a note at Plains Heritage, Highway 58, Dannebrog, NE 68831, or even better yet at captneb@micrord.com. I try to answer each and every letter I get—before I lose it in this mess I call a desk. Also, drop by and visit our Web site at http://www.agriculture.com/welsch/roger/. There is a catalog there of my other books, if you liked this one.

And I want to thank all of you. Writing doesn't amount to much if there isn't someone reading at the other end of the process. I very much appreciate your interest and support and look forward to meeting you here again, in the pages of a book or *Successful Farming* magazine.

Roger Welsch